Western Educational Philosophy

Western Educational Philosophy

Dr. Ismail Thamarasseri

GenNext Publication

First Published, 2019

Published by

GenNext Publication
5, Ansari Road
Daryaganj, New Delhi-110002
Phone: 9811692060
E-mail: gennextpublication@hotmail.com

Printed at: G. Print Process, Delhi.

Cataloging in Publication Data—DK
Courtesy: D.K. Agencies (P) Ltd. <docinfo@dkagencies.com>

Thamarasseri, Ismail, author.
Western educational philosophy / Dr. Ismail Thamarasseri.
pages cm
Includes bibliographical references and index.
ISBN 9789380223520

1. Education—Philosophy. I. Title.

LCC LB14.7.T43 2019 | DDC 370.1 23

Contents

Preface

Philosophy is the discipline concerned with questions of importance to us which we cannot answer through empirical observation. These include how one should live (ethics), what sorts of things exist and what are their essential natures (metaphysics), what counts as genuine knowledge (epistemology), and what are the correct principles of reasoning (logic). The word itself is of Ancient Greek origin; A compound of philía (love) and sophía (wisdom). The philosophy of education is a significant area of study both for Western and Indian philosophers. Philosophy of education was not systematically set forth before the twentieth century. In the Plato produced a notable philosophy of education (in his "Republic") in pre-twentieth century. He was the first systematic philosopher to work in this field. Plato along with John Dewey believes that philosophy of education occupied a central place in philosophical thought. Dewey, in fact, once suggested that "philosophy may even be defined as the general theory of education."

It cannot be denied that different places have their own different culture and backgrounds. Generally, a Western philosophy of education comprises two schools, which are traditional and modern. It has its roots in Athens, Rome and Judeo-Christianity, whereas Eastern philosophy is derived from Islam, Confucianism, Taoism, Hinduism and Buddhism. By looking at Eastern and Western countries, both have distinct differences in their ways of developing and shaping an individual, in terms of skills and attitudes. Thus, different cultures will have different philosophies, which results in different ways of doing things, especially in educating the next generation.

The idea and the notion of philosophy of education has been derived traditional and modern, became combined and simultaneously work on each other, in order to produce the supreme culture of education to the humanity. Discussing on this discipline, there are numerous aspects that are not parallel with each other, whenever comparing these aspect within the understanding of education itself, through the countries apart of this global nation. The culture and tradition of the society itself had shaped in development of philosophies. This book will look on the Western Education Philosophies from the aspect of students involvement within classroom activity, the techniques of teaching and learning process, the expression of learning process, the capability of students for philosophies, the encouragement for the students, and the relationship between the teachers and the students.

In preparation of this book the author had to refer to the works of other authors and information sources. The author feel a deep sense of gratitude for incorporating their ideas in the text. The author extremely indebted to various authors, editors, educationists and scholars whose views and opinions are integrated in this book. The author shall ever remain obliged to his teachers, parents, friends, colleagues, family members and students for their kind directions, guidance and assistance. The author takes this opportunity to express his sincere thanks to Prof. N.A. Nadeem, Prof. Nighat Basu, and all staff members of the Central University of Kashmir for their valuable support. To them all, the author offer his grateful thanks to ***M/s. GenNext Publication New Delhi*** who came forward willingly undertakes the publishing of this book.

Dr. Ismail Thamarasseri

October, 2018

Srinagar, J&K

Chapter - 1

Philosophical Basis of Education

Introduction

Philosophy is the study or creation of theories about basic things such as nature of existence, knowledge and thought or about how people should live. **Philosophy of education** can refer to either the academic field of applied philosophy or to one of any educational philosophies that promote a specific type or vision of education, which examine the definition, goals and meaning of education. **Philosophy** determines whether the aim of education should be intellectual, spiritual, liberal, aesthetic, moral or vocational. The teacher must possess a sound philosophy of life. The educator must be a lover of wisdom, a seeker of knowledge and a individual of virtues and values. Then only the educator bring about desirable changes in the pupils.

As an academic field, philosophy of education is the philosophical study of education and its problems and its central subject matter is education, and its methods are those of philosophy. The philosophy of education may be either the philosophy of the process of education or the philosophy of the discipline of education. That is, it may be part of the discipline in the sense of being concerned with the aims, forms, methods, or results of the process of educating or being educated; or it may be meta-disciplinary in the sense of being concerned with the concepts, aims, and methods of the discipline. As such, it is both part of the field of education and a field of applied philosophy, drawing from fields of **metaphysics**, **epistemology**, **axiology** and the **speculative**, **prescriptive**, and **analytic** philosophical approaches to address questions in and about pedagogy, education policy, and curriculum, as well as the process of learning, to name a few. For example, it might study what constitutes upbringing and education, the values and norms revealed through upbringing and educational practices, the limits and legitimization of education as an academic discipline, and the relation between educational theory and practice.

The multiple ways of conceiving education coupled with the multiple fields and approaches of philosophy make philosophy of education not only a very diverse field but also one that is not easily defined. Although there is overlap, philosophy of education should not be conflated with educational theory, which is not defined specifically by the application of philosophy to questions in education. Philosophy of education also should not be confused with philosophy education, the practice of teaching and learning the subject of philosophy. Philosophy of education can also be understood not as an academic discipline but as a normative educational theory that unifies **pedagogy**, **curriculum**, learning theory, and the purpose of education and is grounded in specific metaphysical, epistemological, and axiological assumptions. These theories are also called educational philosophies. For example, a teacher might be said to follow a **perennialist** educational philosophy or to follow a perennialist philosophy of education.

Philosophy is a search for a general understanding of values and reality by chiefly speculative rather than observational means. It signifies a natural and necessary urge in human beings to know themselves and the world in which they live and move and have their being. **Western philosophy** remained more or less true to the etymological meaning of philosophy in being essentially an intellectual quest for truth. **Indian philosophy** is intensely spiritual and has always emphasized the need for practical realization of truth. Philosophy is a comprehensive system of ideas about human nature and the nature of the reality we live in. It is a guide for living, because the issues it addresses are basic and pervasive, determining the course we take in life and how we treat other people. Hence we can say that all the aspects of human life are influenced and governed by the philosophical consideration. As a field of study philosophy is one of the oldest disciplines. It is considered as a mother of all the sciences. In fact it is at the root of all knowledge. Education has also drawn its material from different philosophical bases.

Education, like philosophy is also closely related to human life. Therefore, being an important life activity education is also greatly influenced by philosophy. Various fields of philosophy like the **political philosophy**, **social philosophy** and **economic philosophy** have great influence on the various aspects of education like educational procedures, processes, policies, planning and its implementation, from both the theoretical and practical aspects. In order to understand the concept of Philosophy of education it is necessary to first understand the meaning of the two terms; Philosophy and Education.

Meaning of Philosophy and Education

The word philosophy literally means *love of wisdom*; It is derived from two Greek words i.e. 'Philo' (love) and 'Sophia' (wisdom). This tells us something about the nature of philosophy, but not much, because many disciplines seek wisdom. Since times immemorial there have been various pursuits for unfolding the mystery of the universe, birth and death, sorrow and joy. Various ages have produced different thoughts throwing light upon the mystic region. The ultimate truth is yet to be found out. This eternal quest for truth 'lends the origin of philosophy. A love of wisdom is the essence for any philosophical investigation.

On the standard way of telling the story, humanity's first systematic inquiries took place within a **mythological** or religious framework. Wisdom ultimately was to be derived from **sacred traditions** and from individuals thought to possess privileged access to a supernatural realm, whose own access to wisdom, in turn, generally was not questioned. However, starting in the sixth century BC, there appeared in ancient Greece a series of thinkers whose inquiries were comparatively secular. Presumably, these thinkers conducted their inquiries through reason and observation, rather than through tradition or revelation. These thinkers were the first philosophers. Although this picture is admittedly simplistic, the basic distinction has stuck: philosophy in its most primeval form is considered nothing less than secular inquiry itself. The subject of **philosophical inquiry** is the reality itself. There are different schools of philosophy depending on the answers they seek to the question of reality. It is the search for understanding of man, nature and the universe. There are different branches of philosophy-**Epistemology**, **Metaphysics**, etc. There are different fields of philosophy such as **educational philosophy**, **social philosophy**, **political philosophy**, **economic philosophy** etc. There are also different philosophical approaches such as **idealism**, **naturalism**, **pragmatism**, **materialism**, and so on.

Etymologically, the word education is derived from *educare* (Latin) "bring up", which is related to *educere* "bring out", "bring forth what is within", "bring out potential" and *ducere*, "to lead". Education in the largest sense is any act or experience that has a formative effect on the mind, character or physical ability of an individual. In its technical sense, education is the process by which society deliberately transmits its accumulated knowledge, skills and values from one generation to another. Webster defines education as the process of educating or teaching. Educate is further defined as "to develop the knowledge, skill, or character". Thus, from these definitions, we might assume that the purpose of education is to develop the knowledge, skill, or character of students. In ancient Greece, **Socrates** argued that education was about drawing out what was already within the student. The **Sophists**, a group of **itinerant teachers**, promised to give students the necessary knowledge and skills to gain positions with the city-state. Thus we see that there are different views and understandings of the meaning of the term education.

In the modern times it has acquired two different shades of meaning namely: (1) an institutional instruction, given to students in school colleges formally ;and (2) a pedagogical science, studied by the student of education. Education is the dynamic or practical side of philosophy. Philosophy takes into its orbit, all the dimensions of human life. Similarly education also reflects the multifaceted nature of human life. Therefore, education is closely related to various aspects of human life and environment. Hence, the term education has a wide connotation. It is difficult to define education by single definition. Philosophers and thinkers from Socrates to **Dewey** in west and a mass of Indian philosophers have attempted to define education. However education can be understood as the deliberate and systematic influence exerted by a mature through instruction, and discipline. It means the harmonious development of all the powers of the human being; physical social, intellectual, aesthetic and spiritual. The essential elements in the educative process are a creative mind, a well-integrated self, socially useful purposes and experience related to the interests of the individual, needs and abilities of the individual as a of a social group. In the historical development of man, education has been the right of a privileged few. It is only in recent centuries that education has come to be recognized as a human right. All have equal right to be educated as education has become prerequisite of civilization.

Concept of Philosophy of Education

All human societies, past and present, have had a vested interest in education; and some intellect have claimed that teaching is the second oldest profession. While not all societies channel sufficient resources into support for educational activities and institutions, all at the very least acknowledge their centrality and for good reasons. For one thing, it is obvious that children are born illiterate and innumerate, and ignorant of the norms and cultural achievements of the community or society into which they have been thrust; but with the help of professional teachers and the dedicated amateurs in their families and immediate environs within a few years they can read, write, calculate, and act in culturally-appropriate ways. Some learn these skills with more facility than others, and so education also serves as a social-sorting mechanism and undoubtedly has enormous impact on the economic fate of the individual. Put more abstractly, at its best education equips individuals with the skills and substantive knowledge that allows them to define and to pursue their own goals, and also allows them to participate in the life of their community as full-fledged, autonomous citizens. Equips individuals with the skills and substantive knowledge that allows them to define and to pursue their own goals, and also allows them to participate in the life of their community as full-fledged, autonomous citizens.

But this is to spread matters in very individualistic terms, and it is fruitful also to take a societal perspective, where the picture changes somewhat. It emerges that in pluralistic societies such as the Western democracies there are some groups that do not wholeheartedly support the development of autonomous individuals, for such folk can weaken a group from within by thinking for themselves and challenging communal norms and beliefs; from the point of view of groups whose survival is thus threatened, formal, state-provided education is not necessarily a good thing. But in other ways even these groups depend for their continuing survival on educational processes, as do the larger societies and nation-states of which they are part; for as **John Dewey** put it in the opening chapter of his classic work *Democracy and Education* (1916), in its broadest sense education is the means of the social continuity of life. Dewey pointed out that the primary ineluctable facts of the birth and death of each one of the constituent members in a social group make education a necessity, for despite this biological inevitability of the life of the group goes on. The great social importance of education is underscored, too, by the fact that when a society is shaken by a crisis, this often is taken as a sign of educational breakdown; education, and educators, become scapegoats. It is not surprising that such an important social domain has attracted the attention of philosophers for thousands of years, especially as there are complex issues aplenty that have great philosophical interest.

Abstractly, at its best education equips individuals with the skills and substantive knowledge that allows them to define and to pursue their own goals, and also allows them to participate in the life of their community as full-fledged, autonomous citizens. But this is to cast matters in very individualistic terms, and it is fruitful also to take a societal perspective, where the picture changes somewhat.

It emerges that in pluralistic societies such as the Western democracies there are some groups that do not wholeheartedly support the development of autonomous individuals, for such folk can weaken a group from within by thinking for themselves and challenging communal norms and beliefs; from the point of view of groups whose survival is thus threatened, formal, state-provided education is not necessarily a good thing.

The following are some issues that philosophers have deeply thought about and philosophy is still in the process of answering these questions. Is Education as transmission of knowledge versus education as the fostering of inquiry and reasoning skills that are conducive to the development of autonomy; the question of what this knowledge, and what these skills, ought to be two sets of issues that relate to the question of the capacities and potentialities that are present at birth. The tension between liberal education and vocational education, and the overlapping issue of which should be given priority be given educational programs that differ in content or in aims; the issue of whether the rights of children, parents, and socio-cultural or ethnic groups, and a set of complex issues about the relation between education and social reform, centring upon whether education is essentially conservative, or whether it can be an agent of social change.

It is here that philosophy of education plays an important role in providing direction to education on the following issues as well as providing a theory of knowledge for education to work upon. Philosophy of education is essentially a method of approaching educational experience rather than a body of conclusions. It is the specific method which makes it philosophical. Philosophical method is critical, comprehensive and synthetic. Therefore, (1) Philosophy of education is the criticism of the general theory of education, (2) It consist of critical evaluation and systematic reflection upon general theories and (3) It is a synthesis of educational facts with educational values. In brief, it is a philosophical process of solving educational problems through philosophical method, from a philosophical attitude to arrive at philosophical conclusions and results. Thus, it aims at achieving general as well as comprehensive results.

New Perspectives in Philosophy of Education

The chief task of philosophy is to determine 'what constitutes a life worth living'. The chief task of education is 'to make life worth living'. Therefore the relationship between philosophy and education is very close. Philosophy tells the goal and essentials of good life. Education tells the means to achieve those goals and learn those essentials of good life. Philosophy deals with abstract; education deals with the concrete. All great philosophers are great educators. Fichte says; "The art of education will never attain complete clearness without philosophy". James Ross remarks; "Education is the dynamic side of philosophy". John Dewey observes; "Philosophy is the theory of education in its most general phases".

The scope of philosophy of education is confined to the field of education. Thus, it is philosophy in the field of education. The scope of philosophy of education is concerned with the problems of education. These problems mainly include; (1) interpretation of human nature, the world and the universe and their relation with man, (2) interpretation of aims and ideals of education, (3) the relationship of various components of the system of education, (4) relationship of education and various areas of national life like economic system, political order, social progress, cultural reconstructions etc. (5) educational values, and (6) theory of knowledge and its relationship to education. The above mentioned problems constitute the scope of philosophy of education and explain its nature.

The desire to seek a grounding for philosophy of education in philosophy meant that more and more scholars, including students studying for graduate degrees in the field, went into philosophy departments or the relevant aisles in libraries and bookstores and started reading work in **existentialism**, **phenomenology**, and other ***Continental philosophies***. It meant that many philosophers of education read or re-read primary sources in philosophy and looked increasingly outside Anglo-American philosophy to more international sources. They also turned to texts on the margins of what had been counted as "philosophy" before: critical theory, **feminism**, and those who would later be termed "**postmodern**" writers. Their scholarship made substantial contributions to understanding such topics as power and inequality in education, and the critique of cultural intolerance in both the **tacit and the "hidden" curricula**. In many ways returning to the older vision of philosophy of education as necessarily implicated in issues of politics, critique, and reform, these philosophers eschewed the methods of analysis but, even more profoundly, rejected its vision of philosophy of education as an exercise in rational or objective reconnaissance.

Jonas Soltis offered his widely accepted characterization of philosophy of education in 1971 than, within a year, essays were already appearing with titles like "Analytic philosophy of education at the crossroads" (1972). Criticisms of analytic philosophy, some though not all from critical theory or feminist points of view, gained wider credibility during this decade. These criticisms included, chiefly, the question of *whose* concepts were being taken for granted; the criticism that the methods of analysis, ostensibly neutral and objective, in fact imported substantive value commitments; the argument that the view of language undergirding this method was culturally bounded and a historical; and the complaint that its focus on "merely verbal" concerns often made its results trivial and irrelevant. The second generation of analytic philosophers like **Robert Ennis** and **Harvey Siegel** made substantial contributions to understanding issues of critical thinking, the forms of knowledge, and philosophical problems in educational research.

Summary

Philosophy influences every aspect of education namely the aim, content, method and discipline. It is philosophy which determines whether the aim of education should be intellectual, spiritual, liberal, aesthetic, moral or vocational. For example, the Hindu philosophy in ancient India resulted in the evolution of the *Gurukula* system of education. The militant philosophy ancient Sparta gave rise to the regimental system of education. The Nazism of Germany gave rise to the Fanatic, anti-Jewish system of education. Philosophy influences the methodology too. **Naturalistic philosophy** emphasizes child-centred methods, **idealism** emphasis **Socratic** and lecture methods.

Pragmatism emphasis the project method. In the case of curriculum, naturalists start with present experiences and interests of children. Idealists stress the study of religion, culture ethics and literature. Pragmatists advocate the study of functional subjects which have utility value. Philosophy influences the discipline in education. Autocratic philosophy leads to repressions, idealism leads to impressionism, naturalism leads to emancipation and modern pragmatism leads to free discipline. The educator must possess a sound philosophy of life. The educator must be a lover of wisdom. Then only they can bring about desirable changes in the future generations.

Model Questions

1. 'Education is the dynamic side of philosophy'. Discuss.
2. Discuss and elucidate, "All educational questions are ultimately questions of philosophy".
3. Discuss the relationship between Philosophy and teaching and teaching styles.
4. "The scope of philosophy of education is unlimited". Critically evaluate this statement.
5. What is the meaning of the term philosophy?
6. Why is an understanding of education philosophy essential for school teachers?
7. Why is the study of philosophy important to education?
8. Why should a teacher study philosophy of education?

Reference

1. Aggarwal, J.C. (1992). *Theory and Principles of Education*. New Delhi: Vikas Publishing House (P) Ltd.
2. Chakraborty A. K. (2003)." Principles and Practices of Education." Meerut, Lal Book Depot.
3. Chandra S. S., R. Sharma, Rejendra K (2002) "Philosophy of Education." New Delhi, Atlantic publishers.
4. Chaube, S.P. & Chaube, A. (1987). *Foundations of Education*. New Delhi: Vikas Publishing House (P.) Ltd.
5. Conner D.J.O. (1957). *An Introduction to the Philosophy of Education*. London: Routledge Kegan Paul.
6. Hospers, John (1953). *An Introduction to Philosophical Analysis*. London: Prentice Hall.

7. http://en.wikipedia.org/wiki/Philosophical_method
8. http://en.wikipedia.org/wiki/Philosophy_of_education
9. http://faculty.education.illinois.edu/burbules/papers/phed.html
10. http://www.mu.ac.in/myweb_test/ma%20edu/M.A.%20Edu.%20 Philosophy.pdf
11. http://www.objectivistcenter.org/cth—409-FAQ_Philosophy.aspx
12. Stanford Encyclopaedia of Philosophy: www.plato.stanford.edu/
13. Thamarasseri, I. & Sabu, S. (2010) *Thoughts on Education*. New Delhi: Kanishka Publishers
14. Thamarasseri, I. (2007) *Education in the Emerging Indian Society*. New Delhi: Kanishka Publishers
15. Thamarasseri, I. (2014). *Philosophical Foundations of Education*. Agra: Shri Vinod Pustak Mandir.
16. The Center for Dewey Studies: www.siu.edu/~dewyctr/
17. www.educao.pro.br/;links.htm

Chapter - 2

Educational Philosophy as a Discipline

Introduction

Some people think that the philosophy of education is the most important aspect of teacher training. Others claim it is so far removed from classroom practice that it is a waste of time. This lesson explaining the value of educational philosophy as an academic discipline. The philosophy of education is important because it explains how educational theories arise. By examining the philosophy of education, we are able to see why and how theories complement or oppose each other. An understanding of philosophy is therefore useful in guiding and critiquing the development of educational theory. Philosophical knowledge may provide a justification for teaching methodologies; reveal and challenge assumptions about the nature of teaching; and provide a language for educational debate. Further, philosophy is vital for the promotion of teaching as a scholarly and professional activity. Education has only recently been recognized as a subject in its own right. Many educational theories are drawn from other disciplines, and a philosophy of education can provide a pedagogical history of ideas, theories and vocabulary. It helps to place the educational discipline on a similar philosophical footing to other disciplines through the establishment of a distinct discourse and rationale.

The concept of education and philosophy form the basis of arriving at the definition of philosophy of education. Thus philosophy of education is essentially a method of approaching educational experience rather than a body of conclusions. It is the specific method which makes it philosophical. Philosophical method is critical, comprehensive and synthetic. Therefore philosophy of education is the criticism of the general theory of education. Clarification of the definition of education will be further clarified by a discussion of scope and nature of philosophy of education.

The traditional concept of philosophy has been developed for ages with reference to **metaphysics**. It deals with the knowledge of the universe, the ultimate reality and its source or origin. Thus philosophy directs its enquiry in to life in its totality. It also deals with the aim and purpose as well as some other relevant issues and problems around life. The task of philosophy is also to unfold the mystery behind creation and the creator.

Philosophy is a term which is based on the concept of life and knowledge. It is an attempt to understand the world of experience in different perspective. "The nature and functions of philosophy itself a kind of philosophical problem over which there have always been controversies" says Reid. Philosophy is lone of wisdom needed most in our life. A philosopher is the lover of wisdom who can see life steadily as a whole. O'conner believes, that is a mistake to assume that philosophy is a sort of superior and profounder science. Metaphysics has emerged as a separate branch of knowledge to explain life and its purpose. Philosophy helps man to attain a clear and consistent conception of world system.

Education is the core of almost all the social sciences. This is a purposive activity, a process and not a product. One can ask if education should have some ultimate objectives. The basic query is whether education should have a philosophy. It does not mean that it should be bound by some set of values. Philosophy provides a vision and a wide perspective.

To **John Dewey**, education is life itself, and it is as dynamic as living. As we live, we learn and educate themselves. This is a **pragmatic** view of Dewey. Various schools of philosophy have emerged with their distinct bearing on education. It appears that education should be consistent with certain fundamental value in life. The question arises whether these dimensions of life, can be reached through education. It is obvious that goodness and truth cannot be divorced from beauty and happiness. Education for happiness is the ultimate concern of all.

Plato provides us with the **psychology** of education. Plato does not forget that life has more than single purpose which a man may consciously pursue. As there are in main reason, spirit and desire, each of these must be developed by training and education. Life in order to have meaning and direction should be guided by philosophy.

Philosophy as a vision helps us to look at life and creation in wider perspectives. Metaphysics in the opinion of **Ewing**, helps one to make genuine discoveries of truth. In short, philosophy of education is the application of philosophy and its methods in the field of education. Education is a purposive activity towards the objectives determined primarily by philosophy. It is a process of enabling one not merely to line but to live adequately. There are various aspects of education, academic, aesthetic, moral, physical, social and spiritual. Theories of education have been formulated and different values emphasized. It is not very difficult to trace the evolution of educational theories.

Epistemology and Education

The most important branches of philosophy are **metaphysics, epistemology** and **axiology**. Epistemology is concerned with the discussion of the problems concerning knowledge. It is analysis of the nature of knowledge. Epistemology or the theory of knowledge has often been thought to be at the heart of the philosophical enterprise. Etymologically, epistemology means, the logic of understanding (episteme) i.e., the origin, nature and validity of knowledge. If you have to know that you have good reasons for a belief before you claim knowledge then it seems that the definition is question-begging. We have two ways for accepting this definition. (1) asking questions and (2) justification of questions.

While most beliefs have to be justified by other beliefs there must be some basic, foundational beliefs which do not stand in need of justification. Epistemology as a distinct branch of philosophy developed out of the growth of **individualism**. Epistemology is the branch of philosophy which is concerned with the discussion of the problems concerning knowledge. Its main problems are: (a) What is the relation between the knower and known? (b) Is the content of knowledge identical with the external object or is it different from it? (c) How can we know that our knowledge is real knowledge of the object? (d) What are the limits of knowledge? and (e) What are the sources of knowledge? etc.

Besides, the epistemologist raises certain other questions such as: what is knowledge? How can we distinguish between true an false knowledge? What is ignorance? Is it a form of knowledge or different from it? What is the process of knowledge? What is the meaning of forgetting of knowledge? What are the errors possible in the process of knowledge? How is it that some beliefs are considered to be more valid than others? What are the distinctions between different types of knowledge? What are the relations of knowledge with science and philosophy?

Epistemology is the philosophical discussion of problems related to knowledge. It uses the philosophical methods of induction and deduction, synthesis and analysis. One finds different conclusions presented by different epistemologists regarding epistemological problems. According to the **realist** philosophers, knowledge is the knowledge of objects, idealists define it as the knowledge of ideas. Some epistemologists think that the presence of object is necessary for knowledge, and therefore, every knowledge is a knowledge of both knower and known; others think that the knowledge of known is different from the knowledge of knower. About the possibility of knowledge, one finds different approaches such as **agnostic**, **skeptic** and **mystic**. All these approaches have thrown light on different aspects of knowledge.

This explanation shows the importance of epistemology for education. **Empiricist school** of philosophy discussed the methods and value of empirical knowledge. Its opposite rationalist school pointed out how some of the knowledge is innate. Scepticism shows the limits of knowledge. **David Hume** pointed out that certainty can be possible only in mathematics and not in the field of sciences. **Agnosticism** shows the relativity of human knowledge. Criticism shows that knowledge is synthetic, requiring sensibility, understanding and reasoning. Intuitionism shows that intellect and intuition are complementary. **Mysticism** shows the value of spiritual experience in the field of religion. **Instrumentalism** points out that reason is an instrument for the satisfaction of human needs. **Humanism** shows that the criterion of all knowledge is man himself and there is no ultimate knowledge. **Experimentalism** and **relativism** points out that knowledge is experimental and relative. This all the schools of epistemology show the methods, limits and value of knowledge. They supply the necessary foundation for all knowledge, scientific and otherwise.

Human knowledge as it exists today broadly consists of facts and theories. New facts, new concepts, and new ways of doing things increased its quantum with the passage of time. This knowledge enables us to understand, comprehend, explain, control, predict or cope with a given situation. The sources from which we obtain knowledge range from those that are highly reliable to those that are completely unreliable. The knowledge obtained from the unreliable sources is based on assumptions, beliefs and untested generalizations. Such generalizations are usually accepted on faith, tradition, or authority and no effort is made to verify their validity. In contrast, reliable knowledge is based on objective verification of generalizations.

The acquisition and expansion of knowledge is not an automatic and self-perpetuating process. On the contrary, it requires constant and planned effort by intelligent and highly trained people. The present level of knowledge is an outcome of the various methods adopted by man over a period of several centuries. The word "know" is slippery. It is not always used in the same way. Sometimes when we take about knowing, we are referring to acquaintance of some kind. For example, "Do you know Mr. Vinod Kumar?" means approximately the same as "Are you acquainted (familiar) with Vinod Kumar?" You might know him, in the sense of acquaintance, without knowing much about him.

Sometimes we speak of knowing how: Knowing how is an ability-we know how to rich a horse if we have the ability to ride a horse, and the test of whether we have the ability is whether (in the appropriate situation) we can perform the activity. The word know is most frequently used in the prepositional sense. E.g. I know that I am an Indian citizen where the word "that" is followed by a proposition.

Metaphysics and Education

Aristotle developed the study of metaphysics to the studied after **physics**. While physics studies the laws of the external form of existence, metaphysics thinks over the real essence of things. Its main problems are: what is the nature of existence? what is reality? what is birth? what are its different forms? is the world one or many? what is time? what is substance? what is causality? what is fact? what is the purpose or aim? what is change? what is novelty? what is similarity? who am I? is there a purpose in creation? is the world determined or free? is there a god? has the world progressed? etc. thus the subject matter of metaphysics includes the self, the world and the god. its scope includes **ontology**, philosophy of self, cosmology and theology.

Metaphysics in brief deals with reality in man, world and hereafter. This has a close learning upon the aims and ideals of education. The metaphysical attitude provides the educationists the proper perspective for devising aims ideals of education. What we want to make out of man depends upon his nature and place in the universe. Again, the concept of self is the basis of the developments of character, the central aim of education, **know thyself** and be thyself is the universally acknowledged aim of education. The concept of world is directly concerned with the individual's relationships with society and nature. While Indian philosophy emphasizes harmony between man and the world, the western philosophers have made too much of man's desire to overpower nature. While the former philosophy has been the foundation of educational institutions like *Vishwabharati* or Sri Aurobindo's institute, the other approach is the philosophy behind the technological and scientific education of today.

In fact, the more integral is the world-view the more multi-sided will be the education based upon it. In the end, moral and religious education is based upon it in the end, moral and religious education is based upon the metaphysical concept of god. This does not mean that moral education must necessarily be linked to **religious education**. It only shows that our explanation of the ultimate reality or the total reality, call it god or anything else, has important bearing upon education particularly its aims and ideals and therefore its means and plans.

The most important metaphysical theories which have influenced education are **Naturalism, Idealism, Pragmatism** and **Realism**. Naturalism has been manifests in different types of theories such as atomic naturalism. Scientific naturalism, mechanistic and historical naturalism. The most important metaphysical theory in the field of education is idealism. Idealism has been subjective, objective, phenomenalistic and absolute. The most influential metaphysical theory in today's field of education, however is pragmatism. This is closely linked to **instrumentalism** and **humanism**. In the end, the metaphysical theory known as Realism is very much influenced by education concerning science and technology.

Axiology and Education

Roy Wood Sellers says, "Philosophy is a collection of sciences such as theory of knowledge, logic cosmology, ethics and aesthetics, as well as a unified survey". **Axiology** is concerned with value theory and attempts to prescribe what is good and right conduct. The subdivisions of axiology include three normative sciences, viz. Logic, Ethics and Aesthetics.

The term **logic** is derived from the Greek word 'logos', which means reason or expression of reason in words. Thus, the etymological meaning of logic is the science of reasoning or argument. According to John Dewey and Stebbing, reasoning is reflective thinking and reflective thinking is a process of finding ways out of some difficulty or problem by weighing the evidences on the basis of a tentative hypothesis and thereby reaching a conclusion. Thus, logic is concerned with the rules or patterns of correct and valid thinking and it examines the rules of valid inferences that enables us correctly to frame our propositions and arguments. In logics, in order to form a conclusion or valid inference inductive reasoning and deductive reasoning is used. Inductive reasoning moves from particular to generalizations and deductive reasoning moves from general statements or principles to particular instances and application. In logic, we study the general principles governing both inductive and deductive reasoning. In short, logic is the basic of all knowledge and it studies various intellectual processes such as thinking, reasoning and judgment. The knowledge of logic helps us in avoiding error and arriving at correct generalizations in every field of knowledge.

Ethics is known as moral philosophy. Ethics is also considered as the science of character or habit because habits and behaviour are related to the permanent peculiarities of human character and conduct is the mirror of character. In a general way, 'Ethics' refers to the philosophic study of moral values and conduct. It consider the duty of human beings and pronounces ethical decision upon conduct. Therefore ethics studies what is right and what is wrong in character. It studies the ideals of human life and shows what ought to be done and what ought not to be done. According to J.S. Mackenzie, "ethics can be defined as the study of what is right or good in conduct". In this definition, ethics has been accepted as the study of both right and good. But there is difference between right and good. The word right is derived from the Latin word 'Rectas' which means "straight or according to law" and the word 'good' is derived from German word 'gut' which means useful for the 'supreme good'. Thus ethics is the study of good behaviour which leads to supreme good.

As a subdivision of axiology, ethics is not true from criticisms. A classical conflict in values between objective versus subjective value theory exists there. There who subscribe to an objective value theory assert that what is good is rooted in the universe itself and is applicable everywhere for all time. According to J.S. Mackenzie, the study of ethics is classified into four divisions, such as; (1) Psychology of ethical consciousness, (2) Sociology of an ethical life, (3) Theories of ethical criterion and (4) Application of ethical criterion in ethical life. These four divisions of ethics are the foundation of all education. As the science of character, ethics analyses the psychology of ethical consciousness. It shown how different moral norms evolve in different circumstances and examines the validity of these norms and provides solid basis for social ethics of the students. Ethics also examines the theories of moral standard and helps in the application of moral principles in actual life. Ethical activities are accompanied by vice and virtue and ethics details the criterion for this vice and virtue.

The aim of education is to realize all-round development of the students. In this development, moral and aesthetic developments occupy foremost place. **Aesthetics** is concerned with the study of values in the realm of beauty and art. It is the science of beauty, as logic is the science of truth and ethics is the science of good. In the broadest sense, aesthetic theory refer to the cultivation of taste and a feeling for that which is beautiful. While moral development requires knowledge of ethics, aesthetics development training in aesthetics. Aesthetics is the basis of all literacy and artistic criticism and supplies the philosophical basis to literature and art. As literature and art contribute significantly to education, the value of aesthetics in education is clear and education seeks to realize the true, the good and the beautiful. In short, aesthetic theory is not only concerned with the human attempt to objectify insights and feelings in various art forms but also equally concerned with the cultivation of persons whose live are harmonious, balanced and beautiful.

Summary

The most widely accepted aim of education is man making and character building and the basis problem of education is to secure humanbeings' fullest development. For this, it is necessary to know what is man, his nature, his sociability etc. The social philosophy analyses human nature and finds out how far man is naturally social and how far not. The social philosophy examines the basic principle of human behaivour and supreme values of human life. Thus, it is the philosophical foundation which provides a solid ground for the educational system. The most important branches of philosophy are metaphysics, epistemology and axiology. Again, the relationship of philosophy and education should be sought in different fields of education such as the aims and ideals, the methods of teaching, the curriculum, the school administration, discipline and finally evaluation. All these branches of education are based upon philosophical foundations.

Model Questions

1. How philosophy determines education?
2. Write a short note the influence of metaphysics on education.
3. What are the three branches of philosophy?
4. What are the three divisions of axiology?
5. How aesthetics and education related?
6. What are the main problems of Epistemology.

References

1. Chandra, S.S. & Sharma, R. (1996). *Philosophy of Education*. New Delhi: Atlantic Publishers.
2. Chaube, S.P. & Chaube, A. (1987). *Foundations of Education*. New Delhi: Vikas Publishing House (P.) Ltd.
3. Conner D.J.O. (1957). *An Introduction to the Philosophy of Education*. London: Routledge Kegan Paul.
4. http://clioetcetera.com/2014/07/19/is-education-an-academic-discipline/
5. http://clioetcetera.com/2014/07/19/is-education-an-academic-discipline/
6. http://education.stateuniversity.com/pages/2321/Philosophy-Education.html
7. http://faculty.education.illinois.edu/burbules/papers/phed.html
8. http://link.springer.com/article/10.1007%2Fs11217-007-9049-z
9. http://onlinelibrary.wiley.com/doi/10.1111/j.1741-5446.1953.tb01057.x/pdf
10. http://oregonstate.edu/instruct/ed416/PP3.html
11. http://plato.stanford.edu/entries/education-philosophy/
12. http://www.mheducation.co.uk/openup/chapters/9780335226702.pdf
13. http://www.tandfonline.com/doi/abs/10.1080/03075077812331376306?journalCode=cshe20
14. https://en.wikipedia.org/wiki/Philosophy_of_education
15. Monroe, Paul (2001). *Encyclopaedia of Philosophy of Education*. New Delhi: Cosmo Publications.

16. Robert R. Rusk. *The Philosophical Base of Education*. University of London Press.
17. Sharma, R. (2000). *Text book of Educational Philosophy*. New Delhi: Kanishka Publishers.
18. Thamarasseri, I. (2007) *Education in the Emerging Indian Society*. New Delhi: Kanishka Publishers
19. Thamarasseri, I. (2014). *Philosophical Foundations of Education*. Agra: Shri Vinod Pustak Mandir.
20. Venkateswaran, S. (1993). *Principles of Education*. New Delhi: Vikas Publishing House (p) Ltd.

Chapter - 3

Functions of Educational Philosophy

Introduction

Philosophy is a rational thought about all issues that influence human life. Have you ever realized that you have certain beliefs and opinion based on important ideas such as the purpose of life, purpose of education, a need for religion, if any, and your destiny, for instance? Have you taken your time to analyze possible basis for the beliefs and opinions you hold? Such beliefs control and create a pattern in your life and an attempt to understand the assumptions on which they are based creates a philosophy. As you analyze and question your beliefs and the basis of the systems in which they are rooted, you generate your personal philosophy. It is possible that you have done so, either consciously or subconsciously. To philosophize, therefore, is to use reason to ascertain the efficacy of principles that govern your belief systems. As you study this lesson, you will be encouraged to enjoy philosophical deliberation by questioning the assumptions upon which important decisions are based. The lesson sets the stage for sustaining a questioning attitude in order to, not only, understand the educative process but also justify its theory and practice.

According to **John Dewey**, philosophy of education is not an external application of readymade ideas to a system of practice having a radically different origin and purpose, it is only an explicit formulation of the problems of the right mental and moral attitudes in respect to the difficulties of contemporary social life. The most penetrating definition of philosophy of education which can be given is, then, that it is the theory of education in its most general phases.

Teaching methods are very much concerned with the philosophy of education the teacher holds. According to **Herbert Spencer**, only a true philosopher may give a practical shape to education. How he behaves with the students and how he communicates depends very much on low he defines the learners. Different philosophical systems of education have explained human nature in widely different ways. This very much governs the teachers attitude to the method of teaching.

In the words of **Bertrand Russell**, "philosophy is to be studied not for the sake of any definite answers to the questions, but rather than the sake of questions themselves; because the questions enlarge our conception of what is possible, enrich our intellectual imagination and diminish the dogmatic assurance which closes the mind against speculation but above all because through the greatness of the universe which philosophy contemplates, the mind also is rendered great and becomes capable of that union with the universe which constitutes its highest good".

The most important contribution of the philosophy of education to the teacher is, however, concerned with the aims and ideals of education. Without philosophy of education the teacher will not have any sense of purpose in his teaching. This is not possible by science; however, we may eulogies the role of science in the present day education. In fact, while science supplies the means, only philosophy supplies the ends. In the words of **John Dewey**, "philosophy is concerned with determining ends of education, while the science of education determines the means to be used"

Again, philosophy of education helps the teacher in the determination of the **curriculum** of education. Plato said, "He who has a taste for every sort of knowledge and who is curious to learn and is never satisfied may be justify termed a philosopher". Philosophy provides a comprehensive and total view of educational situation. It leads to an integral approach. It is a total view point.

Functions of Educational Philosophy

Philosophy of education performs various functions. They are discussed below:

Determining the aims of education: Philosophy of education provides original ideas regarding all aspects of education particularly educational aims. It is said that educational philosophy gives different views, but this situation is not harmful, rather it helps in providing education according to the need of society. The difference in view of philosophy of education reflects the multiplicity and diversities of human life. Philosophy of education guides the process of education by suggesting suitable aims from the diversities of life and selecting the means accordingly.

Harmonizing old and new traditions in the field of education: In the process of social development the old traditions become outdated for the people. They are replaced by the new traditions. But this process of replacement is not always smooth. It is faced with lots of opposition from certain orthodox sections of the society. At the same time it must be kept in mind that every 'old' is not outdated and every 'new' is not perfect Therefore, there is a need of co-coordinating the two in order to maintain the harmony between both. This function can be performed by philosophy of education.

Providing the educational planners, administrators and educators with the progressive vision to achieve educational development: Spencer has rightly pointed that only a true philosopher can give a practical shape to education. Philosophy of education provides the educational planners, administrators and educators with the right vision which guides them to attain the educational goals efficiently.

Preparing the young generation to face the challenges of the modern time: Social commentators have given many labels to the present period of history for some it is the information age and for others it is post modernity, later modernity, high **modernity** or even the age of uncertainty. One more addition to this list may be that 'present age is an age of **Globalization** as a phenomenon arrived on the economic scene in the 1990 in India. This watchword has had its implications in the social political, economic fabric of the country of which education is a part. Philosophy of education is a guiding, steering and liberating force that helps young people to and society at large to face the challenges of the modern time.

Speculative, Normative and Analytical Philosophy

The speculative function of educational philosophy is closely related to its function of determining the values which education ought to pursue. Taken together, these aspects of educational philosophy would seem to indicate that it has a prospective reference and that it anticipates and directs practices. While there are many who agree that philosophy should provide certain ideas at which teachers should aim, there are others who take a less ambitious view of educational philosophy. Philosophy is retrospective rather than prospective in character.

Normative philosophers advocates the aim of education as follows, "the prime goal of education is the conquest of internal and spiritual freedom to be achieved by individual persons". Normative philosophers stresses to three things. (1) What human dispositions are excellences and worthy at cultivation, they will show, (2) Why these dispositions are to be considered as excellence, and they may also discuss, and (3) How these excellence are to be cultivated. **Plato** was one of the normative philosopher.

Analytical endeavour in crucial in philosophy. Concepts control in important lines of enquiry have been clarified. The validity of argument have been assessed, and hidden assumptions have been exposed. **Plato** in ***Republic*** to clarity the concept of justice, he depicted the **Socrates** as taking pains to compose weakness of counter argument at in the dialogue. Contemporary philosophers have attempted to clarify concepts such as 'equity', teaching, learning, punishment, indoctrination, intelligence and education itself.

The Future of Educational Philosophy

Today, this reflexive awareness of how such philosophical boundaries also have institutional effects, and how these boundaries of inclusion and exclusion, in turn, feedback on which philosophical issues and perspectives are or are not represented within what officially counts as "philosophy of education," has ushered in a new period for the field. A diffuse focus, or lack of focus, can be characterized just as accurately as a period of experimentation and expansion in philosophy of education. The contemporary situation is complex, and relatively healthy – philosophers are working with a variety of approaches, in a variety of fields, and the discipline is marked by an **eclecticism** perhaps unrivalled in previous periods.

There are paired centripetal and centrifugal forces at work in the field today, matching philosophers of education who prefer to draw the boundaries of the field more narrowly, around a strict disciplinary view of philosophical method, and those drawing the boundaries more broadly, blurring distinctions of philosophy and theory, and emphasizing the interdisciplinary cross-fertilization of philosophy with literary interpretation, political theory, women's studies, and other fields.

A related issue about such boundary-drawing is the effect of the **professionalization** of philosophy of education upon the involvement of philosophically minded practitioners and their concerns. One can say that philosophers of education should continue to focus on issues of educational practice, this position stands in tension with actual policies that discourage the participation of those who hold these concerns closest to heart. This tension is expressed in the uncomfortable, and occasionally alienated, relation between the philosophers.

As a result of these dynamics, philosophy of education is once again in a period of self-examination about its scope and mission. If disciplinary boundary-drawing is regarded with more suspicion today, and if any prospective philosophical criteria for what counts as "philosophy of education" have come to be scrutinized partly in terms of which voices and perspectives they privilege and which they disadvantage or exclude, then the only alternative demarcations of the field must be more procedural and "boot-strapped." In this sense, philosophy of education today represents those engaged in ongoing conversations, in person or in print, about certain issues, in full awareness of their diversity and **eclecticism** of method, while retaining a degree of openness about who else might need to be drawn into those conversations.

Within this decentred characterization of philosophy of education, what trends stand out for the future? Without stipulating what the changing boundaries of the field will look like, are there good guesses that can be offered about the future of philosophy of education? One avenue, is to recognize how current topics of interest such as identity, difference, power, a suspicion toward "meta-narratives," and so on, have become not only issues for philosophical investigation, but leverage points for reflection and critique within the field of philosophy of education itself.

As the boundaries of philosophy of education are being stretched and blurred, considerations of their role in including and excluding participation are becoming a topic of explicit, reflexive concern. If all criteria exclude someone, then the question of which exclusions will be found liveable, and which ones not, is an element in weighing their relevance and merit.

Methods of Acquiring Valid Knowledge

We are now ready to consider some aspects of knowledge. A proposition may be true although one does not know it to be true. By what means, then, do we come by knowledge? What are the avenues by means of which we are enabled to know propositions to be true? Let us now consider some alleged.

Sense-experience

You can know many things about the world by seeing, hearing, touching, smelling and testing. It is primarily through seeing about touching that we know 'that' physical thing exists. We see the chair and then we sit on it. But all our senses on various occasions inform us of 'what' the thing's characteristics are: we can see the colour and feel the texture of the chair. Sometimes we have sense experience when there is nothing at all to be perceived: We may be having a hallucination, such as when we are thirsty and think we see water and trees in the desert. Sometimes, what we see is really there, but we think it has one characteristic when it really has another: E.g. In the darkness we mistake donkey for a horse. If we are colour blind, we think it is gray when it is black or brown. These are all perceptual errors. The existence of perceptual errors shows that our senses are fallible. When we make a perceptual error owing to incomplete or fragmentary sense-experiences, it is always further sense experience that lead us to discover our error.

Before being embodied into knowledge all sense-experiences require judgement. You must first judge that this is a chair, this is a book and so on. The sense experience itself is neither true or false, it merely exists or occurs. We get information about the outside world- through '**external senses**'. There are '**internal senses**' acquainting us with our own internal states like Feeling, attitudes, moods, pains and pleasures as well as our own mental operations such as thinking, believing and wandering. In these cases we do not have sense organs. We are entitled to state certain prepositions on the basis of certain experiences. E.g. You are thinking about your next summer vacation.

Reasoning

Reasoning is one source of knowledge. It is the degree of ability to engage in thinking. If we could not think, we could not acquire any knowledge. This ability is indispensable to having knowledge of any sort, including knowledge acquired through sense-perception. People are engaged in reasoning when they take certain statements as the basis for making one or more other statements. The most familiar kind of reasoning which is often taken as the model for all reasoning, is **deductive reasoning**. In a deductive argument, the conclusion must logically follow from the premises. If the premises of argument are true, the conclusion must be true.

We also argue inductively: we may know the truth of the premises, but we still do not know the conclusion is true- the premises provide evidence for the conclusion, but not complete evidence. In

inductive reasoning a conclusion is reached by observing all instances and generalizing from instances to the whole phenomena. In order to attain inductive conclusion, all instances must be observed. It is **perfect induction**. To examine all the instances of a phenomenon under study is not practical; one may arrive at a generalization by observing only some instances that make up the phenomenon. This is known as **imperfect induction**. Although imperfect induction does not help man to arrive at infallible conclusions. It can provide him reliable knowledge upon which he makes reasonable decisions.

Authority

The statements we hear or read would require years of investigation before their truth could be ascertained. So as a practical expedient, we usually take the author's word. The modern man seeks advice from authorities for the solution of the problem faced by him. The authorities may be the persons who have had long experience with the problem and who have studied and thought much about it. When factual evidences cannot be obtained to solve a problem, one may have to rely upon authoritative opinion temporarily as the only possible method for arriving at a solution. In such a solution care must be employed in choosing authorities and evaluating their claims to knowledge. One should check not only the credentials of authorities but also the arguments and evidence upon which they base their judgements. The precautions for selecting authority are; (1) The person whose word we take as authority must really be an authority, one who is a specialist in his field of knowledge. (2) Whenever one accepts another person's statement as authority, he should be able to find out whether the authority's statement is true, if he were to take the time and trouble.

Intuition

The word **intuition** is verbally indefinable. The word in its most limited sense is merely the label for a certain kind of experience, one that is not easily described. A conviction of certainty comes upon quite suddenly, like a 'light' going on inside or like a 'flash'. The existence of intuition as an experience can hardly be doubted, doubtless we all have had experiences that we would call intuitions.

It is noted that much of what we claim to know by intuition is actually not this, but through sense- experience. i.e., intuition with knowledge. If you say "I know by intuition", this really does not explain how you know you may arrive at a correct conclusion and not know how you come by it. This is simply a cover up term for our ignorance, revealing only that we do not know how he was able to do this.

Revelation

Sometimes one claims to know something by means of **revelation**. When a person had some experience, he calls it as 'a revelation from God. Whenever something is revealed through a sacred book, the revelation is form God, but through a book. The book is sacred because the author of the book claims that it is true. There are competing candidates for the position of true revelation - **The Bible**, **The Quran, Gita** and numerous other works. If the claims made are such that sense- experiences or reason could substantiate them, then it is because of this we believe that the claims are true, but we could never verify them.

Experience

Our own personal experience or that of others is the most primitive and yet the most familiar and fundamental source of knowledge. In ancient times, nomads and various tribes from their personal experience remembered that certain wild fruits always made them ill, that grains ripened at particular times of the year etc. When confronted with a problem, modern man often tries to seek its answers from his own personal experience or from others who are familiar with the problem. Children often consult their teachers, parents or even their old siblings to derive answers to their questions.

Let us concluding, true knowledge was due to the operation of stable, universal, self consistent being, falsity to an intermixing of becoming non-being, particularly and mere potentiality. All portions of modern philosophy which discuss the possibility, nature and limits of knowledge or the basis of these presuppositions constitutes epistemology.

Summary

Education is a growing science and its foundations are to be explored for a study of the subject as an inter-disciplinary approach. Philosophy is the corner stone of the foundation of Education. But this does not mean that education should be enslaved to philosophy or some set of values created by human society. Philosophy should be interpreted as a vision in a wider prospective. This being so, education should be wedded to some philosophy in general. We need some frames of reference in which education has to fit. There have been various schools of philosophy presenting their views with much optimism. Education is the process of enabling people not merely does live but to live adequately. There are various facts of education: academic, aesthetic, moral, physical, social and spiritual. Theories of education have been formulated and different values emphasized. Every educational practice is illuminated with the backdrop of philosophy. The speculative, normative and critical function of philosophy affects not only the direction of moral guidance that the teacher gives but also affects the direction of moral guidance that the teacher gives but also affects the direction and the emphasis of the curriculum, the colour of the teachers attitudes from day to day, even from hour to hour.

Model Questions

(1) Describe the functions of educational philosophy.

(2) "Philosophy is concerned with ends of education, while the science of education determines the means". Elucidate.

(3) Philosophy of education performs various functions. Which are they?

(4) How philosophy harmonizing old and new traditions in the field of education?

(5) How philosophy providing vision for educators to achieve educational development?

(6) Is education preparing the young generation to face the challenges of the modern time? Substantiate.

References

1. http://clioetcetera.com/2014/07/19/is-education-an-academic-discipline/
2. http://clioetcetera.com/2014/07/19/is-education-an-academic-discipline/

3. http://education.stateuniversity.com/pages/2321/Philosophy-Education.html
4. http://faculty.education.illinois.edu/burbules/papers/phed.html
5. http://link.springer.com/article/10.1007%2Fs11217-007-9049-z
6. http://onlinelibrary.wiley.com/doi/10.1111/j.1741-5446.1953.tb01057.x/pdf
7. http://oregonstate.edu/instruct/ed416/PP3.html
8. http://plato.stanford.edu/entries/education-philosophy/
9. http://www.mheducation.co.uk/openup/chapters/9780335226702.pdf
10. http://www.tandfonline.com/doi/abs/10.1080/03075077812331376306?journalCode=cshe20
11. https://en.wikipedia.org/wiki/Philosophy_of_education
12. Noddings, Nel (1995). *Philosophy of Education* (Boulder, Colorado: Westview Press).
13. Phillips, D.C. (1985). "Philosophy of education," in T. Husen and T. Neville Postlethwaite, eds., *The International Encyclopedia of Education* (Oxford: Pergamon Press) 3859-3877.
14. Phillips, D.C. (1994). "Philosophy of education: Historical overview," in T. Husen and T. Neville Postlethwaite, eds., *The International Encyclopedia of Education, 2nd edition* (Oxford: Pergamon Press) 4447-4456.
15. Philosophy of Education, Nicholas C. Burbules, Department of Educational Policy Studies, University of Illinois, Urbana/Champaign
16. Robert R. Rusk. *The Philosophical Base of Education*. University of London Press.
17. *Routledge International Companion to Education*, Bob Moon, Miriam Ben-Peretz, and Sally Brown, eds. (New York: Routledge, 2000), 3-18.
18. Russel, B. Wisdom of West. London Allen and Unwin.
19. Schofield, H. (1972). *The Philosophy of Education*. London: George Allen.
20. Seetharamu, A. S. (1989). Philosophy of Education. New Delhi, ' Ashish Publishing House.
21. Sharma, R. (2000). *Text book of Educational Philosophy*. New Delhi: Kanishka Publishers.
22. Thamarasseri, I. (2007) *Education in the Emerging Indian Society*. New Delhi: Kanishka Publishers
23. Thamarasseri, I. (2014). *Philosophical Foundations of Education.* Agra: Shri Vinod Pustak Mandir.
24. Vekateswaran, S. (1993). *Principles of Education*. New Delhi: Vikas Publishing House (p) Ltd.

Chapter - 4

Scope and Value of Philosophy of Education

Introduction

The scope of philosophy of education is confined to the field of education. Thus, it is philosophy in the field of education. The scope of philosophy of education is concerned with the problems of education. These problems mainly include; (1) interpretation of human nature, the world and the universe and their relation with man, (2) interpretation of aims and ideals of education, (3) the relationship of various components of the system of education, (4) relationship of education and various areas of national life like economic system, political order, social progress, cultural reconstructions etc., (5) educational values, and (6) theory of knowledge and its relationship to education. These problems constitute the scope of philosophy of education and explain its nature. Thus, the scope of **philosophy of education** includes following.

Aims and Ideals of Education Philosophy

Education critically evaluates the different aims and ideals of education. These aims and ideals have been propagated by various philosophers in different times. They are character building, man making, harmonious human development, preparation for adult life, development of **citizenship**, utilization of leisure, training for **civic life**, training for **international living**, achieving social and **national**

integration, scientific and technological development, education for all, equalizing educational opportunities, strengthening democratic political order and human source development. These and other aims of education presented by educational thinkers in different times and climes are scrutinized and evaluated. Thus, philosophy of education critically evaluates different aims and ideals of education.

Interpretation of Human Nature

A philosophical picture of human nature is a result of the synthesis of the facts borrowed from all the human science with the values discussed in different normative, sciences. The philosophical picture, therefore, is more broad as compared to the picture of man drawn by **biology**, **sociology**, **psychology**, **economics** and **anthropology** and other human sciences.

Educational Values

Value is typically a philosophical subject since it is more abstract, integral and universal. Philosophy of education not only critically evaluates the values but also systematizes them in a hierarchy. Educational values are determined by philosophical values. Educational values propagated by different philosophers have been derived from their own world, view and their outlook on the purpose of human life. Therefore, a scrutiny of the world views, outlook and beliefs is the specific function of philosophy and it is necessary for the philosophical treatment of the values.

Theory of Knowledge

Education is related to knowledge. It is determined by the source, limits, criteria and means of knowledge. The discussion of all these falls within the jurisdiction of **epistemology**, one of the branches of philosophy, therefore, an important area of the functioning of philosophy of education is related to theory of knowledge.

Relationship of education and various area of national life

One of the most important contributions of the philosophy of education to the cause of education is the provision of criteria for deciding the relationship of **State** and education, economic system and education, **curriculum**, school organization and management, discipline etc. These problems have led to the evaluation of different philosophies of education. The criteria of judgment everywhere are determined by philosophy; therefore, philosophy of education provides the criteria for critical evaluation and judgment in these fields.

Value of Philosophy of Education

Philosophy of education is one of the areas of applied philosophy. There are three branches of philosophy namely 'metaphysics, epistemology and axiology. **Metaphysics** is a branch of philosophy that investigates principles of reality transcending those of any particular science. It is concerned with explaining the fundamental nature of being and the world. *Metaphysics* is the study of the nature of things. Metaphysicians ask what kinds of things exist, and what they are like. They reason about such things as whether or not people have free will, in what sense abstract objects can be said to exist, and how it is that brains are able to generate minds.

Axiology is the branch of philosophical enquiry that explores: (1) *Aesthetics*: the study of basic philosophical questions about art and beauty. Sometimes philosophy of art is used to describe only questions about art, with "aesthetics" the more general term. Likewise "aesthetics" sometimes applied even more broadly than to "philosophy of beauty": to the "sublime," to humour, to the frightening—to any of the responses we might expect works of art or entertainment to elicit. (2) *Ethics*: the study of what makes actions right or wrong, and of how theories of right action can be applied to special moral problems. Sub disciplines include meta-ethics, value theory, theory of conduct, and applied ethics.

Epistemology is the branch of philosophy that studies knowledge. It attempts to answer the basic question: what distinguishes true (adequate) knowledge from false (inadequate) knowledge? Practically, this question translates into issues of scientific methodology: how can one develop theories or models that are better than competing theories? It also forms one of the pillars of the new sciences of cognition, which developed from the information processing approach to psychology, and from artificial intelligence, as an attempt to develop computer programs that mimic a human's capacity to use knowledge in an intelligent way. When we look at the history of epistemology, we can discern a clear trend, in spite of the confusion of many seemingly contradictory positions. The first theories of knowledge stressed its absolute, permanent character, whereas the later theories put the emphasis on its relativity or situation-dependence, its continuous development or evolution, and its active interference with the world and its subjects and objects. The whole trend moves from a static, passive view of knowledge towards a more and more adaptive and active one.

The different branches of philosophy overlap one another. A philosopher considering whether people ought to give excess wealth to the poor is asking an ethical question. However, his investigations might lead him to wonder whether or not standards of right and wrong are built into the fabric of the universe, which is a metaphysical question. If he claims that people are justified in taking a particular stance on that question, he is making at least a tacit epistemological claim. At every step in his **reasoning**, he will want to employ **logic** to minimize the chance of being led into error by the great complexity and **obscurity** of the questions. He may very well look to some of the ethical, metaphysical, and epistemological writings of past philosophers to see how his brightest predecessors reasoned about the matter.

Aspects of each branch of philosophy can be studied in isolation, but philosophical questions have a way of leading to other philosophical questions, to the point that a full investigation of any particular problem is likely eventually to involve almost the whole of the philosophical enterprise. One view on education believes or subscribes to the view that philosophy of education comes under the umbrella of axiology. As a branch of philosophy it utilizes philosophical methods for the solution of philosophical problems with a philosophical attitude to arrive at philosophical conclusion. In this comprehensive process it includes facts concerning education and synthesizes them with values. The other school of thought believes that education as a discipline utilizes or needs to incorporate all modes of philosophical inquiry; metaphysical, axiological and epistemological. As individuals involved in the process of education right from the aims, purpose, functions and building theory we need to look at any body of knowledge or generate new knowledge based on the three modes of philosophical inquiry.

Philosophical Method

Philosophical method or philosophical methodology is the study of how to do philosophy. A common view among philosophers is that philosophy is distinguished by the ways that philosophers follow in addressing philosophical questions. There is not just one method that philosophers use to answer philosophical questions. Some common features of the methods that philosophers follow include: (1) A systematic process of being sceptical about the truth of one's beliefs called **Methodical Doubt**. (2) Provide an **argument** or several arguments supporting the solution and (3) Present the solution and arguments for criticism by other philosophers, and help them judge their own called **Dialectic**.

Doubt and the sense of wonder

Plato said that "philosophy begins in wonder", a view which is echoed by Aristotle in his *Metaphysics*: "It was their wonder, astonishment, that first led men to philosophize and still leads them." Philosophizing may begin with some simple doubts about accepted beliefs. The initial impulse to philosophize may arise from suspicion, for example that we do not fully understand, and have not fully justified, even our most basic beliefs about the world.

Formulate questions and problems

Another element of philosophical method is to **formulate questions** to be answered or problems to be solved. The working assumption is that the more clearly the question or problem is stated, the easier it is to identify critical issues. A relatively small number of major philosophers prefer not to be quick, but to spend more time trying to get extremely clear on what the problem is all about.

Enunciate a solution

Another approach is to enunciate a theory, or to offer a definition or analysis, which constitutes an attempt to solve a philosophical problem. Sometimes a philosophical theory by itself can be stated quite briefly. All the supporting philosophical text is offered by way of hedging, explanation, and argument. Not all proposed solutions to philosophical problems consist of definitions or generalizations. Sometimes what is called for is a certain sort of explanation - not a causal explanation, but an explanation for example of how two different views, which seem to be contrary to one another, can be held at the same time, consistently. One can call this a philosophical explanation.

Justify the solution

An argument is a set of statements, one of which, it is said or implied, follows from the others. One might think of arguments as bundles of reasons followed by the claim they are reasons for. The reasons are the premises, the claim they support is the conclusion; together they make an argument. **Philosophical arguments** and justifications are another important part of philosophical method. It is rare to find a philosopher, particularly in the Western philosophical tradition, who lacks many arguments. Philosophers are, or at least are expected to be, very good at giving arguments. They constantly demand and offer arguments for different claims they make. This therefore indicates that philosophy is a quest for arguments. A good argument may ultimately cure the original doubts that motivated us to take up philosophy. If one is willing to be satisfied without any good supporting reasons, then a Western philosophical approach may not be what one actually requires.

Philosophical criticism

In philosophy, which concerns the most fundamental aspects of the universe, the experts all disagree. It follows that another element of philosophical method, common in the work of nearly all philosophers, is philosophical criticism. It is this that makes much philosophizing a social endeavour. Philosophers offer definitions and explanations in solution to problems; they argue for those solutions;

and then other philosophers provide counter arguments, expecting to eventually come up with better solutions. This exchange and resulting revision of views is called dialectic. **Dialectic** is simply philosophical conversation amongst people who do not always agree with each other about everything.

Motivation

Method in philosophy is in some sense rooted in **motivation**, only by understanding why people take up philosophy can one properly understand what philosophy is. People often find themselves believing things that they do not understand. For example, about God, themselves, the natural world, human society, morality and human productions. Often, people fail to understand what it is they believe, and fail to understand the reasons they believe in what they do. Some people have questions about the meaning of their beliefs and questions about the justification of their beliefs. A lack of these things shows a lack of understanding, and some dislike not having this understanding. These questions about are only the tip of the philosophical iceberg. There are many other things about this universe about which people are also fundamentally ignorant. Philosophers are in the business of investigating all sorts of those areas of ignorance. "Methods of philosophy" identify philosophical methodology and the principles it employs in solving problems and resolving issues in human life. There are various philosophical methods are using in education like: Descriptive method, Prescriptive method, Analytic method, Critical method, Phenomenological or reflective method, and Speculative method.

Philosophy of Education and Teaching Styles

Philosophy guides the process of education in different ways. A teacher approaching education philosophically needs to answer four basic questions that guide the teaching learning process. They are: What is the nature of the learner? What is the nature of subject matter? How should one use the subject matter to guide students towards meaningful learning activities? What behaviour trend should one exhibit in order to carry out one's philosophical position? The answers to these questions only will help the teacher to identify a series of preferences, as opposed to a set of behaviour that belong to mutually exclusive categories for the following questions. An attempt to answer these questions is nothing but philosophy of teaching. Philosophy and various philosophical viewpoints inform us that each of these questions have different philosophical perspectives that can be considered as extremes in a continuum.

Nature of the Learner

For the question about the nature of Learner, It will be defined in terms of extremes of the continuum by using the terms - *Lockean* (passive) and - *Platonic* (active). Lockean is a position because it was **John Locke**, in his *Essay Concerning Human Understanding*, who first wrote about mind, is a ***tabula rasa***. He envisioned the operation of the mind as similar to a blank wax tablet on which data taken in through the senses would make impressions. Sensory data which a learner absorbed formed the true source of knowledge. Any complex mental operations involving association, interpretation, or evaluation of secondary data led to the formulation of increasingly complex knowledge. **Platonic** Image is that of a teacher who has so much respect for what the learner can contribute to the learning environment that he or she definitely does not want them to absorb prescribed subject matter, as the teacher sees the subject matter. Under such circumstances learners are viewed as the most important ingredient of the classroom environment because they teach each other and their teacher about problems which are meaningful to them. It is almost that learners have the knowledge which is locked inside them which is released through interaction. Platonic concept believes in the **Doctrine of Reminiscence**.

Nature of Subject Matter

The terms **Amorphous** or Structured are used to delineate extremes on the continuum of teacher's view on the nature of subject matter. The term amorphous label has been reserved for rote learning, which emphasizes that each item to be learned is equal in importance to every other item to be learned ; hence youngsters are not encouraged to find relationships among items to be learned and no item is seen to be more important than the other. The other extreme - **structured**, we may expect to find a position represented by those who have a quite realistic view of what the subject matter can never accomplish. The term *Structured* as used in this context, is from **Jerome S Bruner'**s understanding that any subject matter should be viewed as having a natural structure which can help to explain relationships among its components and which can be used to find new information.

How should Subject matter guide students learning activities?

The two end points of the continuum is **cognitive** and **affective**. These concepts are not mutually exclusive categories, but rather matters of emphasis and preferences. Evidence abounds that students bring into the classroom attitudes which influence the way they perceive facts, concepts and generalizations. Sometimes teachers are fortunate to have students who bring with them positive attitudes towards the subject matter at hand. Most often we have students who bring with them not very positive attitudes. In such situations the teachers' role will be to help students think critically by transforming generalization, beliefs and values into hypotheses that can be tested. Then the teacher resorts to the affective domain.

Behaviour trend in order to carry out one's Philosophical Position

The terms authoritarian and non-authoritarian are two extremes of the continuum, but should be understood as not merely being *stricter permissive*. These words should go beyond the aspect of classroom management as it is more inclusive approach to classroom management. It is an over view of the student and the subject matter which this indicator has been designed to examine. For instance, suppose some teachers encourage students to view subject matter only as experts in that field might view it; hence these teachers habitually accept for each major question under examination only one right answer which all students are excepted to adopt and understand. We can thus say that these teachers are said to encourage convergent thinking and hence in this context we can term them as authoritarian teachers.

The converse can be said of non-authoritarian teachers

Teacher need to be aware of the *Philosophical Positions* that they take and have taken while they enter into classrooms or plan to enter into classrooms. Philosophical positions affect the way they interact with students and facilitate learning in learners individually or collectively. Thus we see that the way we answer the questions of nature of learner, subject matter etc. definitely affects our teaching style. Whether a teacher is authoritative or non-authoritarian, whether teaching methods are constructivist or lecture method are influenced based on the philosophical position that they hold. Therefore, it is essential for the educators to have the deep insight into the philosophy of education.

Summary

Philosophy, life and education are intimately linked with one another. They are also related to time and space. If we consider 'what' 'how' and 'where' to teach, we shall be discussing the subject matter, methods of education and human relations in schools. All these aspects of education are not fixed. They change according to the social and economic needs and concept of social sciences prevailing in our at the particular time. The needs of our present day society are not the same as those of ancient society. The scope of philosophy of education is concerned with the problems of education. The main problems of philosophy of education include aims and ideals of education, analysis of human nature, relationship of education and state, educational values, theory of knowledge and its relationship to education, economic system and education the place of school in educational system the curriculum and process of education, and finally the relationship of education and social progress.

Model Questions

1. Why is an understanding of education philosophy essential for educators?
2. Why Education is the considered as the dynamic side of philosophy?
3. 'Education and Philosophy use like two sides of the same coin'. Elucidate.
4. What is the meaning of epistemology?
5. Why is the study of philosophy important to education?
6. Describe the scope of Philosophy of Education.

References

1. Aggarwal, J.C. (1992). *Theory and Principles of Education*. New Delhi: Vikas Publishing House (P) Ltd.
2. Bourai, H.H.A. (1993). *Indian Theory of Education*. New Delhi: B.R. Publishing Corp.
3. Chandra, S.S. & Sharma, R. (1996). *Philosophy of Education*. New Delhi: Atlantic Publishers.
4. Chaube, S.P. & Chaube, A. (1987). *Foundations of Education*. New Delhi: Vikas Publishing House (P.) Ltd.
5. Conner D.J.O. (1957). *An Introduction to the Philosophy of Education*. London: Routledge Kegan Paul.
6. http://en.wikipedia.org/wiki/Philosophy_of_education
7. http://faculty.education.illinois.edu/burbules/papers/phed.html
8. http://highered.mheducation.com/sites/0072877723/student_view0/chapter9/
9. http://oregonstate.edu/instruct/ed416/PP1.html
10. http://plato.stanford.edu/entries/education-philosophy/
11. http://www.britannica.com/topic/philosophy-of-education
12. http://www.edutopia.org/blog/what-your-educational-philosophy-ben-johnson
13. http://www.mu.ac.in/myweb_test/ma%20edu/M.A.%20Edu.%20Philosophy.pdf
14. http://www.newfoundations.com/EGR/PhilEdCon.html
15. http://www.objectivistcenter.org/cth—409-FAQ_Philosophy.aspx
16. http://www.philosophy-of-education.org/
17. http://www.tc.columbia.edu/arts-and-humanities/philosophy/
18. Monroe, Paul (2001). *Encyclopaedia of Philosophy of Education*. New Delhi: Cosmo Publications.
19. Robert R. Rusk. *The Philosophical Base of Education*. University of London Press.
20. Sharma, R. (2000). *Text book of Educational Philosophy*. New Delhi: Kanishka Publishers.
21. Thamarasseri, I. & Sabu, S. (2010) *Thoughts on Education*. New Delhi: Kanishka Publishers
22. Thamarasseri, I. (2007) *Education in the Emerging Indian Society*. New Delhi: Kanishka Publishers
23. Thamarasseri, I. (2014). *Philosophical Foundations of Education*. Agra: Shri Vinod Pustak Mandir.

24. Vekateswaran, S. (1993). *Principles of Education*. New Delhi: Vikas Publishing House (p) Ltd.

25. www.educao.pro.br/;links.htm

26. www.siu.edu/~dewyctr/

Chapter - 5

Philosophy and Educational Aims and Curriculum

Philosophy And Aims Of Education

Aims, goals, ends or objectives of education are the first essentials of any educational system. Without them the whole educative process would be meaningless. Aims of education depend on the philosophy that prevails at the time of determining the aims of education. That is why they have been changing with the changing philosophy of life. **Acharya J.B. Kripalini**, the noted Gandhian philosopher says; "No System of education, Can be properly appraised, and appreciated, unless it is studied in connection with the ideas and ideals which it represents".

Aims in of education during ancient and medieval period

In ancient times men needed training in the use of bows and arrows for their safety. Their needs were simple and a few. The process of production, consumption, distribution and exchange was quite simple. Thus the educative needs were also simple and could be met by a process of education which was also very simple. Education in Ancient India was mostly dominated by the religious considerations. Learning was considered as a means of salvation or self-realization, **emancipation** has been the highest ends of life.

The aims of Vedic and brahmanical education is that; Emphasis upon knowledge and experience, Sublimation of instincts, Spirituality,

Growth of character and personality, Fulfillment of duty and Protection of culture. Education in the Vedic period meant, an illumination and an agency of improvement. Dr. A.S. Altekar has listed the aims of ancient or Vedic education. They are, Infusion of piety and religiousness, Character formation, Civic and social duties-their inculcation, Promotion of social efficiency and happiness, Development of personality and Spread of culture. Attainment of 'Nirvana' was the ultimate aim of Buddhist system of education. It meant a life of sacrifice and dedication. *Nirvana* was nothing more than this spiritual realization.

Aims of the Medieval Muslim Education was to spread the light of Islam, to infuse the distinct morality in education, to attain material prosperity, and to spread the light of learning and to illuminate the minds of followers of Islam.

Aims in of education during modern times

The Charter Act of 1813 made in English East India Company to accept the responsibility of educating the Indians. Aim of education under British rule mainly was, Produce faithful servants. The aim of education in Free-India changed a lot. Four aims of education stated by the Secondary Education Commission (1952-53) are (1) Development of democratic citizenship (2) Improvement of vocational efficiency (3) Development of personality (4) Development of qualities for leadership.

Education Commission (1964-66) states the objectives of education are (1) Enhancing productivity (2) Strengthening social and national integration through educational programs (3) Consolidation of democracy through education (4) Development of social, moral and spiritual values and (5) Modernization of society. Some of the widely recognized aims of education are listed below.

(a) **Knowledge Aim**: Knowledge lays the foundation of any time of education. Most of the educators in olden days held knowledge as the supreme aim of education.

(b) **Vocational aim**: Education should prepare a child for a vocation or profession, enabling him to earn his livelihood.

Vocational aims are essential for leading a worthy life. A liberal education without vocational education is useless.

(c) **Harmonious Development Aim**: **John Henrich Pestalozzi** and **Mahatma Gandhi** have emphasized 'harmonious development' as an intrinsic quality of any good system of education. Pestalozzi says, "Education as the harmonious development of the heart, head and hand". Gandhi says; "Education is the all-round drawing out of the best in the child and man-body, mind and spirit".

(d) **Complete Living Aim**: **Herbert Spencer** says; "To prepare us for complete living is the function which education has to discharge, and the only mode of judging any educational causes, is to judge in what degree it discharges such function".

(e) **Religious Aim**: Faith in the fatherhood of god and brotherhood of man is the essence of all religion and all religious education.

(f) **Moral Aim**: Herbert Spencer says "the one and the whole problem of education may be summed up in a single concept - **morality**".

(g) **Individual Aim**: Sir Percy Nunn says; "the central aim of education is the autonomous development of the individual", "Nothing good enters into the human world except in and through the free activities of individual men and women. Educational practice, therefore, must be shaped to accord with the truth".

(h) **Social Aim:** Raymont says; "The isolated individual is a figment of imagination". Bagley and Dewey are important advocates of the social aim of education. According to them education should aim at making each individual socially efficient.

Aims of Education in a Totalitarian and Democratic States

J.F. Brown says; "Education in any country and at all periods reflects on the ruling class". The aim of education are determined by the political ideologies. Each individual must be trained to subordinate his interests to the interests of the state. Every child must undergo a rigorous code of discipline. Thinking along the lines approved by the authorities is stressed-very little independent thinking is allowed. Physical education and military training are given great importance. The student is made to realize the value and importance of obedience and conformity.

The aims of education in a democratic setup are (1) It should develop a wide range of whole some interest in each pupil by providing for learning through co-operative work. (2) It should develop social outlook. (3) It should develop ability to constructive and independent thinking. (4) It should develop the capacity of the pupil to different truth from false hood, fact from propaganda, and to reject the dangerous appeal of fanaticism and prejudice. (5) It should provide for training dignity of labour. (6) It should provide equal opportunities to all. (7) It should develop love and respect for others. (8) It should develop human relations. (9) It should cater to the individual difference of children and teach them accordingly. No attempt should be made towards uniformity. (10) It encourages originality and inventiveness and Vocational choices are broad based.

Aim of Education in different schools of philosophies

The **idealistic** aims of education are Exaltation of human personality, Universal Education, Development of inventive and creative powers, Acquisition and enrichment of culture environment, Self realization, Development of moral sense and Self-realization. The **naturalistic** aims of education are Self-expression, Autonomous development of individuality, Improvement of racial gains, and Preparation o the struggle for existence. The **pragmatic** aims of education are Social efficiency, Change with changing times, More and more education and continues growth and Adaptation to environment. According to Realism, the aims of education are Complete living, Understanding of human society, Adjust himself in the environment and develop up to utmost perfection.

Philosophy and Curriculum

The need of philosophy of education felt very seriously in the area of curriculum planning. The philosophical approach to life is the guiding factors in the choice of students to be included in the curriculum. The curriculum is the sum total of the schools efforts to influence learning, whether in the classroom or in the playground, or out of school. K.G. Saiyidain says; "The curriculum is primarily an aid in the process of adjusting the child to the environment in which he functions from day to day and in the environment in which he will have to organize his activities late". The concept of the curriculum differs with different schools of philosophy. According to Idealism curriculum should stress on nature of the child, Curriculum should emphasize the higher values, Curriculum provides humanities a place of prominence, Ethics, religion and arts find an important place. Idealism gives importance to physical education, Hygiene, philosophy, physical skills, gymnastics, and athletics.

Naturalistic Curriculum is based on the nature of the child, his interests. It lays stress on subjects that are helpful in self-preservation. It stresses basic sciences and It emphasis physical and health education. Pragmatism stresses experience curriculum. **Pragmatism** regards utility as the prime mover in the determination of curriculum. Pragmatism assigns due place to the interests of the child and it provides for problem-solving activities. Pragmatism emphasis subjects and studies like physical training, hygiene, social studies, maths and science. The **realist** gives a high priority to subjects like physical sciences and mathematics. Modern languages may find a place in the curriculum because they enable one to read, write and conduct all types of social intercourse; but literature, as such will find no prominent place because the realist believes that it is out of touch with the real line of human advance.

Philosophy and Methodology of Teaching

Methodology of teaching establishes a contact of the teacher, the taught and the subject. It raises many problems. All such questions and the problems that arise in the classroom techniques are satisfactorily tackled by philosophy. The Idealistic Method of Teaching are Learning through reading, Learning through lecturing, Learning through memorization and discussion, Learning through imitation and Socratic method.

Naturalism believes in Learning by doing, Learning through experience, Learning through observation and Learning through heuristic method.

Pragmatic method of teaching getting wide acceptance across the world now a days. These are Project method, Learning by doing, Learning through creative activities, Learning through purposeful activities and Learning through experiences.

The socialist philosophy **Sarvodaya**, is a culmination of Indian and idealistic thought. Its foundation have deep roots in the Indian soil, but it is different from Indian philosophies. Our philosophies were individualistic. Sarvodaya, Its basis in the socio-economic conditions of the present day world, is aimed at the 'good of all' presents a synthesis of all good points in different Indian and western philosophies of life. "Correlation of studies" is the main principle of Sarvodaya method. It develop an integrated personality.

The philosophical method is not absolutely different from scientific method. Philosophical problems have much in common with the scientific problems. The philosopher utilizes the same method of **induction** and **deduction** as used by scientist. The principles of different sciences are arrived at by means of **inductive process**. The philosopher utilizes concepts and propounds new theories. E.g. materialism, idealism etc. And then s/he tries to explain his/her experiences satisfactorily on the basis of these theories. Deduction is the process to arrive at certain particular prepositions from a general prepositions.

Dialectical method is the natural method of philosophical thinking. This is a common place experience that when we think over a problem we arrive at certain positive facts. That is *thesis*. Now after sometimes we came to know some facts which are contradictory to thesis that is *anti-thesis*. This thesis and anti-thesis cannot live together for a long, hence they are synthesized into a *synthesis*. This synthesis arrived through anti-thesis is more comprehensive than the original thesis. Thus knowledge grows in a dialectical process through thesis to anti-thesis and then synthesis. This method was developed by **Hegal.**

Analysis means the process of distinction between different elements evolved in a particular state of experience, so that, they might be more clear. Realistic philosophers have emphasized this procedure while absolutists have advanced arguments against it. **Synthesis** method involves connecting together the scattered elements in a particular experience which brings into light new patterns and facts. The idealist philosophers have laid emphasis on synthesis.

The Methods of Philosophical Analysis

The methods of philosophical analysis were ideally suited to a stance of clear-eyed **skepticism** in the face of educational nonsense; of reasoned, balanced objectivity in the face of highly contested educational disputes; and of providing a helpful, elucidative service that colleagues in education could find amenable to their concerns. Without neglecting the philosophical arguments that were posed in favor of analytic method, to which we will turn in a moment, there can be little doubt that these stances also suited the professional self-interest of a discipline seeking academic credibility as philosophically rigorous, in part through stronger affiliations with professional associations in philosophy. They also reinforced a position of nonpartisanship in the constantly shifting arena of competing educational fads and trends.

Analytic philosophy of education made substantial contributions in elucidating such concepts as "**authority**," "**indoctrination**," and even the terms "teaching" and "education" themselves. This method specialized in offering fine-grained distinctions and typologies; diagnosing hidden equivocations or blurriness in the ordinary concepts found within educational slogans or clichés; and criticizing faulty logic or misleading uses of statistics or other evidence. In many cases, educators found such analyses salutary and helpful: this was philosophy in the service of plain speaking and no nonsense.

This analytic movement within philosophy of education followed developments within Anglo-American philosophy: notably the movement of **logical positivism** and various forms of **linguistic philosophy**. But the arguments raised in favor of analytic methods had the widespread appeal that they did within philosophy of education, in large part, because of their congruence with other imperatives within the field as an increasingly professionalized discipline.

There is a certain ambivalence that has often accompanied philosophy of education: on the one hand seeking credibility in relation to the traditions of philosophy; on the other seeking legitimacy within the often-utilitarian climate of schools of education. This tension tends to pull philosophy of education in competing, incompatible directions and helps to account for what she calls the relentless need to explain and justify the discipline. **Analytic method** seemed to hold promise as the indisputably philosophical core that would controversially link the discourses of philosophy of education with mainstream philosophy. At the same time, its appeal to clarity and logic meant that philosophers of education would not have to endure the accusations of abstraction, obscurantism, and irrelevance they often heard within schools of education.

The rise of analytic method clearly severed the chains joining philosophy of education. While the John Dewey continues, to be read and reread in light of shifting philosophical trends remain a hardy staple of scholarship in the field. The analytic period established the independence of philosophy of education from **Progressivism**.

The analytic movement in philosophy of education took a particular shape in opposition to the movement that had preceded. One of the central tenets of the analytic school, was that there were no direct implications of substantive philosophical positions for education: that a person may believe in Realism, for instance, but still favor any of a variety of educational aims and practices. The attempt to provide encapsulated summaries of complex, difficult philosophical positions, and then to read off from them neat implications for practice, was regarded as being philosophically casual, and as overpromising what philosophy could provide to education.

Perspectives in Philosophy of Education

The philosophical work in education from critical theory or neo-Marxist, feminist, and postmodern perspectives, beginning during this period and expanding to the present day, brought not only a shift in philosophical perspectives and methods, but a more explicitly political commitment. Issues of class, gender, race, and other dimensions of disadvantage and exclusion became explicit topics of investigation and focal points of advocacy. These issues were raised, reflexively, as points of critique against the field of philosophy of education itself. Such manifestations have a dual relation to the scope and content of a field: representing the work with which people are actually engaged, yet also reflecting back to the field what literatures, topics, and perspectives are of current interest or importance. To the extent that scholars are influenced by what they read, such shifting trends play an active part in encouraging and giving legitimacy to new styles of work.

The circular process by which a field becomes what it is thought to be, in the minds of its members is exemplified practically in these activities. For philosophy of education in the post-analytic period, the contents are increasingly eclectic, interdisciplinary, and iconoclastic toward traditional conceptions of the field. That this partly was an indication of a changing state of affairs, and partly a cause of it, was quite apparent to those involved in making such selections.

Something else momentous was happening to philosophy of education during this period is represented by two related sets of changes. The first concerned the **demographics** of the field, especially during the 1970s and into the 1980s, as more and more women entered what had been virtually all-male organizations or, among those women who were already participants, as more shifted their interests away from analytic philosophy or other traditional topics toward women's status within education. The second was the rise of **feminism** as a perspective on philosophical and professional issues within philosophy of education. Feminists pointed out that the questions of who was part of certain philosophical debates, and what philosophical language those debates privileged, were interdependent issues. They argued that the forms of philosophical argumentation, in which rigorous, aggressive debate was assumed to be the best way of testing new propositions, had the effect of narrowing the range of perspectives available for discussion and actively intimidating or silencing those who did not debate their points in that manner. They argued that the methods of analytic philosophy, such as the tendency to isolate conceptual issues from actual contexts, gave artificiality to philosophical discussions, notably in cases of ethics where, they believed, situated, interpersonal factors needed to be topics of philosophical consideration from the very start.

In these and other ways they argued the interdependence of issues of *content* and issues of *representation*. Which philosophical issues were being discussed, how they were discussed, and which issues were never discussed directly influenced and were influenced by the fact of who was part of those conversations, and who was not. The increased **eclecticism** of philosophical sources seen as relevant to philosophy of education, and the increased awareness of the interdependence of issues of content and of representation are fundamentally transforming the field today. In the last decade of the twentieth century, philosophy of education scarcely resembles a discipline with a distinct purpose and a clearly established agenda. It is more accurately characterized as a field of study defined by the variety of its research and interpretive projects.

Summary

Philosophy of education is an important branch of applied philosophy. Of the three divisions of philosophy, meta-physics, epistemology and axiology, philosophy of education falls in the third. It is, therefore, mainly concerned with educational values. As a branch of philosophy it utilizes philosophical methods for the solution of philosophical problems with a philosophical attitude to arrive at philosophical conclusions. In this comprehensive process it includes facts concerning education and synthesis them with values. The horizon of education is gradually expanding the modern movement in education is concerned with the child and its development in relation to his life and environment. Some amount of idealism underlying the philosophy of new education. Today education has become experimental as a science in the laboratory of human life. Principles underlying all the educational behaivour are derived from philosophy of education. Whenever philosophy has been taken seriously it has always been assumed that it signified achieving a wisdom that would influence the conduct of life.

Model Questions

1. How philosophy determines the aims of education?
2. How and why curriculum changes one philosophy to another philosophy?
3. Enlist the idealistic aims of education .
4. Describe the pragmatic methodology of education?
5. Why is the study of philosophy important to educators?
6. Describe the emerging trends of Philosophy of Education.

References

1. Chandra, S.S. & Sharma, R. (1996). *Philosophy of Education*. New Delhi: Atlantic Publishers.
2. Chaube, S.P. & Chaube, A. (1987). *Foundations of Education*. New Delhi: Vikas Publishing House (P.) Ltd.
3. Conner D.J.O. (1957). *An Introduction to the Philosophy of Education*. London: Routledge Kegan Paul.
4. http://ieeexplore.ieee.org/iel5/4703377/4720249/04720417.pdf?arnumber=4720417
5. http://pakphilosophy.blogspot.com/2014/03/idealism-and-aims-of-education.html
6. http://plato.stanford.edu/entries/education-philosophy/
7. http://www.academia.edu/1733948/Aims_of_Education_-_Philosophy_and_education
8. http://www.britannica.com/topic/philosophy-of-education
9. http://www.studylecturenotes.com/social-sciences/education/247-aristotle-theory-of-education
10. https://en.wikipedia.org/wiki/Philosophy_of_education
11. https://sol.du.ac.in/solsite/Courses/UG/StudyMaterial/16/Part1/ED/English/SM-1.pdf
12. https://www.researchgate.net/publication/224361021_Screening_curriculum_aims_and_objectives_using_the_philosophy_of_education
13. https://www2.viu.ca/homeroom/content/topics/programs/aims37.htm
14. Monroe, Paul (2001). *Encyclopaedia of Philosophy of Education*. New Delhi: Cosmo Publications.
15. Robert R. Rusk. *The Philosophical Base of Education*. University of London Press.

16. Sharma, R. (2000). *Text book of Educational Philosophy*. New Delhi: Kanishka Publishers.
17. Thamarasseri, I. (2007) *Education in the Emerging Indian Society*. New Delhi: Kanishka Publishers
18. Thamarasseri, I. (2014). *Philosophical Foundations of Education.* Agra: Shri Vinod Pustak Mandir.
19. Vekateswaran, S. (1993). *Principles of Education*. New Delhi: Vikas Publishing House (p) Ltd.

Chapter - 6

Idealism and Naturalism

General Statement and Tenets of Idealism

Idealism can be discerned in the debates of thinkers from the earliest periods when philosophy emerged as a field of knowledge. The term is derived from idea plus ism, with '*I*' inserted to separate the vowels and effect euphony or good sound effect. Idealism is the philosophy which holds that reality is of the nature of mind. Philosophers like **Hegel** and **Croce** maintain that all genuine philosophy is idealism because the principle in every case is an idea. But the commonsense view of idealism as ideal plus ism also finds many supporters, especially when discussing absolute values. Absolute **truth**, **beauty** and **goodness** can be approached closer and closer, but never fully grasped, at least in finite human experience. **Socrates** held that absolute knowledge cannot be attained by man, but *love of wisdom* or *philosphia* is possible for the person with this deep quest. Besides these views there is also the 'holistic' view of idealism. In Calderwood's view, idealism is "a unifying of reality; a representation of the totality of being as explained under a single conception, or according to an ideal scheme".

Hocking defines idealism as "the philosophy which holds that reality is of the nature of mind". Whereas the sophists claimed to teach particular knowledge, **Plato**'s teacher, Socrates pursued the quest after universal knowledge; this knowledge cannot be 'taught' through external sources; the learner must be helped to 'recollect' the knowledge hidden in his mind, which can be drawn out through the *Socratic dialogue*. The teacher is only a 'midwife' in the birth of knowledge. This knowledge deepens into self-knowledge and broaden out to universal knowledge.

Idealism is one of the oldest schools of thought in the world of philosophy, originating human nature itself, continuing from the primitive man to his present counterpart in some modified form or the other. From the metaphysical standpoint it has overtones of spirituality since it believes that ultimate existing element is spiritual in nature. The entire universe is an extension of the mind or soul. From the epistemological standpoint it is better called idealism, implying there by that thought or idea has greater validity than the physical object. The term idealism cannot different concept when placed in various contexts.

Importance of Idealism

Adams says; "Idealism is one form of other permeates the whole of the history philosophy". GTW Patrick says; "Idealists refuse to believe that the world is a great machine. They deny the supreme importance of matter, mechanism and the conservation of energy, as explaining our world. They feel the somehow certain sciences, such as psychology, logic, ethics, aesthetics, have to do with things intrinsic, that they are quite as much a key to nature's secretes as are physics and chemistry. They believe that the world has a meaning, a purpose, perhaps a goal, and that there is a kind of inner harmony between the heart of the universe and the soul of man, such that human intelligence can pierce through the outer crust of nature and penetrate to its being, at least in some measure". This explanation of idealism highlights its distinction from materialism.

Idealism as the Oldest Philosophy

It is perhaps the oldest philosophy in the world. Many of the world's leading philosophers and educators are idealists. This philosophy continues to extort great influence on education. In the western world idealism began with Socrates and Plato and in the east, it originated from the **Upanishads**. Idealism has been also compared to **realism**. Brubackar says; "Some realists take the view that mental functions can be reduced to bodily ones, while certain idealists make matter a function of the mind. The idealists arrive at their monism by pointing out that it is central in understanding the world". The Chief Exponents of Idealism includes the Vedic sages, Plato (427-347 BC), Kant (1724-1804 AD), Hegel (1770-1831 AD), Froebel (1772-1852 AD), William. T. Haris (1835-1909 AD), Swami Dayananda (1825-1883 AD), Rabinder Nath Tagore (1861-1941 AD) and Aurobindo Ghosh (1872-1950 AD).

Idealism in Education

The idealistic school in education is represented by Plato, Comenius, Kapila, Kant, Pestalozzi, Schopenhaver, Hegel, Froebel, Swami Dayananda, **Rabindra Nath Tagore**, and **Mahatma Gandhi**. All these educational idealists believe that man is born with a spiritual-self. He can realize his spirituality and understand its true nature only through the agency of education. Rusk says, "Education is expected to enlarge the boundaries of the spiritual realm". Idealists also believe that it is through the agency of education that the ideals of race and its cultural pattern are preserved, transmitted and modified subsequently, in the light of new situations.

Idealistic philosophy of education takes various forms. One form of idealism is due to **Hegel**. The other form is due to **Leibniz** and the third form is associated with the name of **Bishop Berkeley**. These three forms assume: (1) Universe is a great thought process. The physical universe is thought made visible. We come into contact with great absolute thought through art, philosophy and religion. (2) Matter is essentially mental or spiritual. Every atom is a psychic entity and has life, mind and energy and (3) Things exist and have reality only when they are perceived by our mind.

The fundamental principles of idealism is (1) Spirit and mind constitute reality (2) Man being spiritual is a supreme creation. (3) God is the source of all knowledge. (4) Values are absolute and unchanging (5) What is ultimately real is not the object itself but the idea behind it and (6) Man is not the creator of values.

The philosophical principles of idealism in education is (1) Stress on spiritual environment (2) Self-realization as the aim of education

(3) Relatively unimportant place for the child in the educative process (4) Development of the child in accordance with adult standards (5) Stress on disciplining the child (6) Emphasis on Book-knowledge (7) Positive education and (8) Education as the dynamic side of philosophy.

Idealistic Aims of Education

Self Realization is making actual or real the highest potentialities of the self. The aim is to enable each one to become his highest and truest self. The goal of educative effort-self realization is meant for all. It is not the prerogative of the few education. The hierarchy of values which help in the process of self realization may be as (i) an appetite for learning, (ii) clear speech, (iii) effective use of health, knowledge and health habits, (iv) recreation, (v) aesthetic interests and (vi) character. Realization of Spiritual Values is another idealistic aim of education. Truth, Beauty, Goodness are the eternal values. One of the main purposes of life is apprehension and appreciation of these values. Each spiritual value is unique and has no equal or parallel.

Idealism expecting enrichment of cultural heritage through education. Religion, morality, art, literature, mathematics and science are the products of humans' moral, intellectual and aesthetic activity throughout the ages. Unfolding of the divine in Man is another idealist aims of education according to Froebel. He says, "The object of education is the realization of a faithful, pure inviolable and hence holy life. Education should lead man to clearness concerning himself, and in himself, and to unity with god". The most important aim of education according to idealism is the development of personality. This has been called man making by **Swami Vivekananda**. Self realization requires development of will power. Synthesis of man and nature aim at achieving an understanding of nature in human beings and educating the learner with the permanent laws which guide and control natural phenomena.

The function of school is not only to transmit the culture from one generation to another, but to provide the individual with conditions to enlarge it further. The transmission will be possible only when more efficient and more economical methods are devised. Self realization can achieved when man realizes his possibilities to recreate and re-acquire the cultural heritage.

General Introduction to Naturalism

At least three varieties of **Naturalism** are current in discussions in educational philosophy. One is designated variously as physical or mechanical naturalism. This coincides mostly with realism except **social realism**, **humanistic realism** and some sophisticated aspects of India realism. Aspects like **sense realism** and even some more refined forms may overlap with this variety of naturalism. The another variety of **biological naturalism** focuses child nature, the child as a growing developing organism, displaying different characteristics according to the level of development. The '**romantic naturalism**' associated with **Jean Jacques Rousseau**.

Many schools of naturalism are a protest against the artificially and complexity of modern society, against the fetters imposed in institutional life, against the aberrations created in 'civilized' life and against the repressions in forced external discipline. They decry the verbalism of the school which substitutes words for things. They demand a going back to the natural way of life, to primal nature itself. Rousseau pictures the 'natural' state of man in glamorous terms as full of joy, freedom and opportunity for healthy natural growth; as an 'integral' as compared with the 'fractioned' social life; as containing all the worth-wile values of life and education, robbed by the so-called civilized life. Nature represents external natural setting, contrasted with the busy city life; it also means child nature, which has its own ways, different from that of adult ways and competencies. These should be respected for the sake of ensuring healthy growth and a sound education. The understanding of child nature and growth patterns have now been taken over by developmental psychologists like Elizabeth Hurlock and others. This aspect may be called biological naturalism. But it was Rousseau who fist called attention to education according the stages of child growth.

The forceful attack on what by the name of education was first exposed in the modern period by Rousseau. The pathology of the school is fully exposed. He attacks the slavishness, conformity, suppression of individuality, cruelty imposed on children by imposing a meaningless curriculum induced by the school claiming to prepare for a future-which is uncertain. This negative critique of the school as later taken up by **Ivan Illich** (*De-schooling Society*), **Pal Goodman** (*Compulsory Mis-education*), **Paulo Freire** (*Pedagogy of the Oppressed*), **Reimer** (*The school is dead*) and others. The concept of direct pedagogy emphasizing impression and instruction is being substituted in naturalistic schools by an indirect pedagogy extolling expression from within.

The concept of education is natural unfolding. Rousseau calls this 'negative education'. In this context 'negative' has a very positive meaning. It simply means that the child has all the potentialities to grow from within and reveal the various competencies in due course. Premature imposition will only spoil the realization of the objectives and yield only half-baked products. The educator's function is to just protect the child from harm and allow him to grow at his own pace.

As against the idealist who claims to have lofty ideals in some mental realm, or the realist who claims to imprint specific objects externally in a on ordered way, Rousseau insists on nature's way in getting the educational outcomes emerging from inside. If at all values are to be seen they have to be sought in nature or in the child. He opens his famous work *Emile* with the statement: "Everything is good as it comes from the hands of the author of nature; everything degenerates in the hands of man". He also holds child nature to be intrinsically good. "The first movements of nature are always right. There is no original perversity in the human heart". The concept of preparation for a distant future emphasized by idealists and realists is questioned. There is nothing more absurd than fixing an objective which is far above the level of child or far distant in terms of time and offering negative external motives or to force him to achieve it. The age of fun should not be spent in the midst of tears, punishments, threats and slavery. Independence and freedom are natural values. All that the school should do is to remove the fetters and constraints. Rousseau says, "Civilized man is born, lives and dies in slavery: at his birth he is wrapped in swathing bands; at his death he is nailed in a coffin; throughout the time he wears the image of man he is bound hand and foot by our institution".

Some people see natural values as 'epicurean values' of "Eat, drink and be merry; for tomorrow we die". This is based on a misunderstanding. **Epicurus** himself led a frugal saintly life, reducing his consumption and wants. Satisfaction of all one's wishes and greed may bring immediate joy but bring suffering as a consequence. Lasting joy is got by controlled natural living. This was the life which Epicurus led and which many 'idealistically' oriented naturalists advocate. Hence natural life is a simple and disciplined life, which helps one to overcome sorrows. Many idealists too share this view.

Naturalistic Education

The naturalist is against an overloaded curriculum imposed externally. For very young children it will take the form of play and other activities suited to the age and environment. It is all the better if chosen by the children themselves. Premature education of the mind is discouraged. Healthy growth of the body will help the growth of the mind and spirit. Externally imposed bookish curriculum is condemned. Rousseau says, "I hate books. They only help one to talk about what one does not know". The only book which Rousseau will allow *Emile* to use is *Robinson Crusoe* – which is a symbol of learning through discovery in natural conditions away from civilized society. The whole design of Emile's education is by self-education in such settings.

Learning should come from things and not from words. When Rousseau said, 'Childhood has its own ways of seeing, feeling and thinking, different from adult ways" and when he said that the educator must 'lose time' rather than 'save time' by keeping the child engaged in doing something in the school (which is beyond his capacity), he was anticipating the modern ideas of **Jean Piaget** and **Maria Montessori**. Montessori's *didactic apparatus* were designed to allow the child to learn arithmetic and reading as his capacity grows without forcing him prematurely. When the time comes the child 'explodes into' arithmetic or reading. In 'losing time' with the apparatus designed by Piaget's disciples instead of doing formal addition, subtraction and multiplication in the lock-step style, the child may be developing schemas far ahead of the child who is doing mechanical arithmetic, and when the schemata are fully formed, he may work very fast and overtake the plodding child who was working mechanically, falsely assimilating higher mental tasks in lower mental **schemata**.

Curriculum different to two stages. In earlier stage nothing to be taught except what the child asks for. Physical activities and health training, play, stories and songs are the early lessons. In this stage importance is given to training of the senses. In later stage, Physiology, Physical Science, Natural Science, Mathematics, Language, Psychology, Social Studies, Anatomy, Study of Nature through manipulation, and exploration of the environment are suggested.

The **naturalistic teacher** must learn the methods not from books, but by observing nature's ways and following her methods. The teacher should not use a level or type of discourse which the child will not understand. The teacher must be a companion, a friendly observer, creating the right conditions for learning in the natural setting. External discipline, especially, punishments and threats, are to be avoided. Rousseau advocates the discipline of natural consequences. If the child breaks the window-pane, the mentor will not punish the child; nor will he replace the glass. The child will catch cold, and Rousseau expects the young child to form the connection between breaking the glass and catching cold.

Another concept of natural discipline is called **emancipation**. Some experiments is Summer-hill and other centers allow boys and girls to mix freely and grow naturally without threats, punishments and unnecessary restrictions. Some of the fears expressed by orthodox people did not come about, at least to the extent anticipated by them. Even Mahatma Gandhi attempted such approaches to some extent at one stage in South Africa. Children growing up naturally under healthy conditions free from threats and unnecessary constraints do not develop repressions or display defense reactions to the extent to which excessive external discipline. Rousseau's powerful critique of educational deviation in his time was instrumental in making education child-friendly, natural, more joyful, and when done in the optimal way even more achieving in the long run. But Rousseau himself did not put his ideas into practice. His own children were admitted in orphanages. It was his disciples, and those influenced by him directly- such as **Pestalozzi**, Froebel and Montessori who gave a positive form to 'negative education', education through free joyous activity, education in natural conditions, Children's garden or Kindergarten etc.

While attaching societal aberrations Rousseau overlooked the positive contributions of society. The cases of children brought up by wolves and away from human interaction shows that the natural man is a fraction, while the social man is a whole. Nature is to be complemented by social and sensible educational action. Rousseau was right in condemning social aberrations which denatured the child. But the outright attack on all social and institutional action was unjustified.

The doctrine of natural consequence may not work with young children who cannot see the connection between their action and the dangerous consequence which will come much later. Even when the connection is made, the child can learn from an experience only if he is alive. The presence of the parents and other adults around the child is also endowed by nature. The natural help which they would render on certain occasions should not be artificially withheld. The free play of natural education, supplemented by judicious social and educational 'intervention', preferably in 'invisible pedagogy' seems to produce optimum results.

Summary

In conclusion, we may say that idealistic philosophy of education stresses the exaltation of human personality through self realization. It emphasis his higher values of life but at the same time, it does not disregard the present life of man. It only advocates that present life is only a means to achieve higher ends. Then it stresses self discipline and the creation of a school environment in which the pupils may willingly behave in a disciplined manner. This philosophy also recommends an ideal teacher who is well equipped. Naturalism does not have the absolute epistemology of idealistic schools. But it questions what goes on in the name of nurturing knowledge in the school. It is sheer verbalism. In fact knowledge unfolds naturally in the child. When it is related to child growth, as done by Rousseau and biological naturalists, it may be treated as an anticipation of the genetic epistemology of Jean Piaget. Nature itself is a value and the matrix in which other values emerge, according to naturalism.

Model Questions

1. Critically evaluate idealist general and educational philosophy.
2. Describe the contributions of Rousseau to educational thought and practice and asses the relevance of the ideas to the education system of the present.
3. How far idealistic philosophy is workable in Indian school? Substantiate your answer with regard to the aim, content and method of this educational philosophy.
4. Mention the educational contributions of Rousseau.
5. Name some of the Idealists.
6. What are the main philosophical ideas of Naturalism?
7. Write a note on the influence of naturalism in modem education.

References

1. Aggarwal, J.C. (2002). *Theory and Principles of Education*. New Delhi: Vikas Publishing House (P) Ltd.
2. Belock & Green J.L. (Ed.). *Philosophy and Education*. Meerut: Any Prakashan.
3. Belock and Green, J.L. *Philosophy and Education*. Meerut: Any Prakashan.
4. Bhattacharya, S. (1996). *Foundations of Education*. New Delhi: Atlantic Publishers and Distributors.
5. http://plato.stanford.edu/entries/idealism/
6. http://plato.stanford.edu/entries/naturalism/
7. http://public.wsu.edu/~campbelld/amlit/natural.htm
8. http://www.britannica.com/topic/idealism
9. http://www.britannica.com/topic/naturalism-philosophy
10. http://www.dictionary.com/browse/idealism
11. http://www.iep.utm.edu/germidea/
12. http://www.iep.utm.edu/naturali/
13. http://www.merriam-webster.com/dictionary/idealism
14. http://www.philosophybasics.com/branch_idealism.html
15. https://en.wikipedia.org/wiki/Idealism

16. https://en.wikipedia.org/wiki/Naturalism_(philosophy)
17. Ismail Thamarasseri & S. Sabu (2010) Thoughts on Education. New Delhi: Kanishka Publishers
18. Ismail Thamarasseri (2007) Education in the Emerging Indian Society. New Delhi: Kanishka Publishers
19. Kneller, G.F. (1971). *Introduction to the Philosophy of Education*. New York: John Willy and Sons.
20. Thamarasseri, I. (2014). *Philosophical Foundations of Education.* Agra: Shri Vinod Pustak Mandir

Chapter - 7

Pragmatism & Realism

Introduction To Pragmatism

Pragmatism is a typical modern philosophy that found its natural expression in the USA. **Kill Patrick** holds that pragmatism is "not so much a new philosophy as a new attitude, a new method of approach to philosophic problem". More than two thousand years ago **Aristotle** took the position that speculative activity, pursued for its own sake is superior to practical activity' in contrast to this view, pragmatism puts emphasis on what is practical, efficient, useful and satisfying. Many philosophers expect to find absolute standards for truth, beauty, goodness. The pragmatists make these relative to human conditions. Absolute 'mansions of philosophy' may look perfect in paper. But they may not be fit for human habitation.

Two antecedents of typical pragmatic elements from antiquity may be cited. One is from ancient Greece. Among the wandering teachers called sophists, who claimed to teach new Athenian youth new things needed to deal with the conditions met with in their time, **Protagoras** has been identified as the greatest. His dictum was 'Man is the measure of all things', thus questioning absolute, unchanging values. In ancient India, the Jain people are thought to have developed an awareness of multiple standpoints, as seen in the story of the six blind men who touched different parts of an elephant and described the elephant differently. Even in talking about the ultimate issues, they developed the *syad vada* or probability discourse. The *syadvada* comes close to the scientists' stand that repeated experimentation increases the probability rather than assure certainly.

Charles Peirce (1839-1914) was the first to use the term pragmatism. It is derived from the Greek root, means, 'active' or 'efficient'. Pierce derived his conception of pragmatism from his theory of meaning. Meaning of an entity is to be derived and tested from its objective and observable consequences from our experience of from controlled experiment. **William James** (1802-1910) was popularized the pragmatism, though not always in the sense in which Peirce intended it.

F.C.S. Schiller (1846-1937) was another who popularized the pragmatism. His views go by the term 'humanism' because of his man-measure theory. The greatest contributor to educational pragmatism was **John Dewey** (1859-1952). He not only contributed to building up his philosophy in several educational contexts, but also helped to test them in his laboratory school. His approach is sometimes called **experimentalism** because he insisted on experimental or experiential testing. It is also called **operationalism**, because hypotheses and action plans are developed through mental operation, and testing is often conducted through physical operations. It also called **instrumentalism**, because philosophy became an instrument in helping to solve problems.

Mind, which was given priority in idealism, and denied by many schools of realism, was seen as instrument in biological adaptation of the human being to his environment. When the tree finds that its supply of water is short, all that it can do is to shed its leaf and prevent further loss of water. Plants in arid zones already have the adaptation to conserve water. The animal can walk to the place where it finds water. Man alone can arrange to bring water to where he is using his physical and mental capabilities, and the tools devised by him.

Educational Implications of Pragmatism

Pragmatism differs from the other schools which first attempt to develop the philosophical principles and then seek applications. Here the principles and applications come together. In fact Dewey holds that education and philosophy are two sides of the same coin. He defines philosophy as 'the general theory of education'. Because of his close relation, inbuilt educational application.

The pragmatist avoids a priori definitions of education. Education starts with experience, is part and parcel of experience, and becomes an attempt at reconstructing experience along widening circles. He finds it easier to say what education does than to say what education is. Dewey says that "the only true education comes through the stimulation of the child's powers by the demands of the social situations in which he finds himself".

Dewey attacks the concept of education as preparation for the future. It does not use children's motive power. Since the work has no relation to the present, children tend to postpone it indefinitely. The right preparation for the future is to make the best of the present. According to Dewey the concepts such as unfolding or drawing out, are not based on the child's initiative. On the positive side, growing is emphasized as the essence of education. Growing is actually 'a continuous leading into the future'. "Life is a self-renewing process through action upon the environment. Continuity of life means continued re-adaptation of the environment to the needs of the living organism". Education is the means of this social continuity of life. Education is also considered as direction. Direction implies that energies are led in a certain continuous course, instead of dispersing aimlessly. In a general sense every stimulus directs activity. Effective direction involves a focusing and fixation of action in order that it may be truly a response, and this requires an elimination of unnecessary and confusing movements". But coercive methods of direction are unproductive. It must be self-direction. If a definition is required education may be defined as a reconstruction of experience.

Pragmatic Curriculum and Methods

The pragmatic theory of curriculum steers clear of the formal training of the mind which gives too little importance to the content, and of the essentialist schools which give too much to it. Dewey seeks to reconcile what others consider contradictory into a **dialectic**.

The child and the subject are simply two poles in the education process. They are not opposed to each other. The curriculum is a dialectical interaction between the two. If the curriculum is translated in terms of the child's experience and maturity level most of the problems would vanish. The pragmatists are against premature *verbalization* and *formalization* of the curriculum, against a wordy knowledge rather than a working knowledge, with young children. With grown up pupils formal statements of the stored knowledge of the race may be appropriate. The pragmatists prefer a situational of a pre-structured or systematic curriculum. The systematic organization of content in the book need not imply that pupils will carry this system in their mind. The classifications and system that pupils themselves make will be most fruitful. It is wrong to divide the subjects as liberal and vocational studies. Work done with intelligence, with relevance can be produce both intellectually and economically. Study can be vocational and liberal at the same time.

Educational methods are not antithetical to matter. According to Dewey, "method is the effective direction of subject matter to desired results. It is antithetical to random and ill-considered or ill-adapted action". Method is based on a reflection upon experience. The demarcation of matter from method results in an isolation, which leads to (1) neglect of concrete situations of experience; (2) false concept of discipline and interest; (3) learning becomes a direct and conscious end in itself; (4) methods are reduced to cut and dry routine, following mechanically prescribed steps.

Inquiry approach and environmental approaches comes naturally to the pragmatist. The typical pragmatic methods include project method and Dewey's activity programme. The project has four steps; purposing, planning, executing and judging; these steps should of the pupil and not that of the teacher. Activity programmes has the following steps: problem, collection and analysis of data, projection and elaboration of suggestions or ideas (hypothesis), experimental action and testing. Here again care should be taken to see that the steps do not become mechanized routine. In each stage the responsibility of the pupil is important.

Discipline, interest and effort

The schools which pitch their target far from the level and interest of pupils have to resort to artificial motivation, and exhortation to put in 'effort'. When this also proves ineffective external disciplining procedures are attempted. In pragmatism, interest, effort and discipline are naturally related. Dewey connects 'interest' etymologically with 'between'. Interest connects things that are otherwise distant. It creates an attitude of concern, of participation. Once the pupil takes interest in the activity, he will be able to put forth more effort in order 'to endure in an intelligently chosen course in the face of distraction'. Thus interest helps to develop genuine discipline in the class. Externally imposed negative discipline will be minimal or totally absent in the pragmatic school.

The pragmatic teacher

The pragmatic teacher does not start with a *pirori* theories or fixed goals. S/he takes life as he finds it. S/he helps pupils to develop their own goals. S/he steps in only when the children cannot do the work by themselves. Even these interventions will be brief and of a catalytic nature. S/he will not consider his work as successful till the pupil is 'liberated from teaching' at least with reference to the specific tasks taken. Gradually the pupils' sense of independence will become general. The pragmatic teacher takes the pupil into confidence in setting up educational goals, in planning, executing and judging. S/ he understands the needs, interests and capacities of each pupils, but not as fixed quantities. S/he respects the freedom of the pupils. S/he is a leader of group activities, but takes care to develop pupil leadership too. S/he is sensitive to the curricular and self-building potentialities in various environmental situations.

General Statement and Tenets of Realism

Realism in its elementary form is the simple philosophy of commonsense. But it tends to be asserted as a school in reaction to (1) extreme subjective idealism which asserts that the objects that we see and touch everyday do not exist except as perceptions in individual minds: (2) the degeneration of idealism to memorization of mere words instead of live wrestling with thought; and (3) the inefficient forms of child-centered, activity-centered pedagogy. The main tenets of commonsense realism are: (a) There is a realm of nature which exists beyond or outside our minds, (b) Nature existed before we knew it, exists whether or not we know it, and will continue it exist after we pass away, (c) The attributes of physical objects exist just as we know them, except for errors of perception which are verifiable as errors. The true nature of a thing is not altered by the mere circumstance of its being known, (d) Experience is the touchstone of what is real, and (e) Physical nature follows or manifests a network of laws.

While realism is so simple for practical purposes, complications arise when we probe into the nature of the reality. Commonsense realism is accepted and tested by physics, and when physics goes deep enough it goes far away from commonsense. Among Indian schools, *Vaiseshika* realism started with commonsense, but in its elaborations reached far beyond commonsense, but revealing a high level of analytical acumen relevant even for modern scientific thought. Before analyzing some typical forms of western and Indian realism, it would be useful to summarize the forms it as taken in its development.

Educational Applications

Realists define education as the conditioning of the nervous system by physical means so as to make it more amenable to physical direction, to make the individual more of a piece with the environment. The realist ideal of education is therefore to open wide the doors of the senses, and to welcome physical reality. **Bertrand Russell** pleads that the individual should mirror the world, as within a camera, to sense the diversified spectacle of nature and the history of humanity. But this mirroring should, be tinged with emotion and with the consciousness of power to change.

The **metaphysics** of commonsense realism accepting the world as real makes it simple and easy to approach educational problems directly. It also helps to correct the escape mechanisms which would follow from some extreme mentalist schools. The Hindu realistic schools are dualistic; they include mind as a sixth sense, besides being and organizing principles. This makes it easy for them to study psychology on same plane with physics. Since *Samkhya* and *Yoga* schools are also dualistic, their educational and general tenets discussed under realism apply here. *Sankhya* philosophy has *prakrti* as the twin initial principle along with *purusa*. The yogi starts with the reality of the physical body and other external factors while on his journey to the final state of 'ecstasy'- the state of peace an calm. The realists believe that reality is a cosmos and is finished.

Realistic Epistemology

The realist theory of knowledge follows from their concept of mind. Drake says, "In physical terms knowledge consists in our afferent and efferent relations to things known, that is, in events in the sense-organs, the neural arcs, and the muscular system". But realists generally believe that explanations and theorization beyond a point can lead us to forget the real fact. The fact is "we know, we know that we know and we know what we know". Retention of knowledge is explained by realists in terms of intensity, decency and frequency. Learning is explained in terms of links or bonds of external association forged through mere repetition. The system of meaning and insight which idealists make much about is explained in terms of familiarity born out of frequent repetition. Realists believe in the correspondence theory of truth. Since the world is a cosmos, it is possible to formulate dependable scientific laws. There is a correspondence between the facts of the outer world and the knowledge, the final court of appeal is the senses, which open the door to the outer world. Hence realistic curriculum is systematic and representative of the world. **Wolfgang Ratke** (1571-1635), one of the earliest to develop realist curricula, emphasized the principle of 'First the thing itself, and then the explanation' and 'All things through experience and investigation'. All the arts and sciences should be taught and the vernacular should be used in teaching.

Aims, Values, Curriculum and Teacher

The realists' statements of aims of education are closely related to the demands of external order to which the pupils have to adjust.

John Locke starts with the dictum of 'a sound mind in a sound body' and gives primacy to the vigour and health of the body. The next aim which he stresses is virtue, which is obtained by the formation of good habits and a long discipline of desires. Various moral traits such as justice, liberality, fortitude, truthfulness, industry and sound breeding are emphasized. Locke also places knowledge as an aim, but with an idealistic tint, emphasizing formal discipline of the mind. The social realists considered education in frankly utilitarian way, as the preparation for the life of 'the man of the world'. The humanistic realist aimed at mastery of life in one's own surroundings natural and social, through a knowledge of the broader life of the ancients.

Herbart Spencer makes moral development the chief aim of education. He also states development of many-sided interest as a related aim. Herbert Spencer also regards moral education as the chief goal of education. His *five subsidiary aims of education* are drawn from the concept of preparation for complete living, i.e., preparation for: (1) direct self-preservation; (2) indirect self-preservation; (3) rearing children; (4) citizenship; (5) ways of spending leisure. This is a typical realistic analysis of the aims, since realists hold existing adult life as the norm for pupils to prepare for. The five-fold preparation analysis also makes out a case for the introduction of science, which was neglected in schools in Spencer's time. Physiology, hygiene, physics and chemistry are necessary for direct self-preservation. Science and arts leading to securing of food, clothing and shelter help indirect self-preservation end so on.

Alfred North Whitehead advocates education for disinterested intellectual curiosity and aesthetic appreciation as educational aims. Bertrand Russell forecasts that science gives increasing evidence that one day man on earth will go to utter destruction. While it lasts, man can have the pleasure of experiencing the splendour of the universe and the enhancing beauty of nature. S/he can enjoy culture and knowledge, strive to obtain peace through the renunciation of futile personal desires. Russell advocates the inculcation of physical health and energy, friendly feeling, appreciation of beauty, enjoying the intrinsic delights of ideas, and independence of thought. Realism, except very modern varieties of the school-presupposes a stable order outside the individual and it tries to reproduce the order of this cosmos in the individual. Hence realists believe in deriving educational objectives through carefully made job analysis and activity analysis of the social and natural environment, word them as behavioural objectives, and organize them systematically in a hierarchy. Statement of objectives in terms of clearly specified terminal behaviours has helped to give concrete shape to the realistic curricula, and facilitated objective evaluation.

The concept of finished cosmos makes the **curriculum and methods** systematic and stable. Their inductive approach invokes them to learn from the external world- either directly through observation, or through the medium of the textbook, models and the teacher. **John Amos Comenius** coined the motto, 'Things before words'. Examples should precede rules. He organized object lessons and prepared illustrated textbooks. **The realist teacher** strives to be clear, systematic and objective and experts his pupils too be or become so. S/he is impartial. S/he holds facts and truth in great regard, and attempts to extend the frontiers of knowledge through exploration of the real environment. As a teacher, however, S/he suppresses his discoverer personality and seeks to let the facts speak for themselves. S/he expects students to deal with the subject themselves in course of time and make their own discoveries. Individual differences among students are studied in a dispassionate way and dealt with on scientific lines.

Summary

The pragmatic theory of truth and knowledge appears to fit well with the experimental temper of modern science, and makes philosophy continuous with science. It provides a framework for fitting in the increasing mass of 'truths' which continue to expand into indeterminacy. It makes the researcher not a mere onlooker, but an active participant in the process, a maker of truth. The realist teacher strives to be clear, systematic and objective and experts his pupils too be or become so. The realist educator suppresses his discoverer personality and seeks to let the facts speak for themselves. In realism, the teacher-student relation is asymmetric. The teacher can be said to have taught only if the student has learnt. But the teacher himself has learnt it prior to the teaching act. Several teaching models have been developed with reference to the teacher-student interaction.

Model Questions

1. Critically evaluate pragmatic general and educational philosophy.
2. Describe the contributions of John Dewey to educational thought and practice and asses the relevance of the ideas to the education system of the modern era.
3. How far pragmatic philosophy is workable in school? Substantiate your answer with regard to the aim, content and method of this educational philosophy.
4. Name some of the pragmatic educational philosophers.
5. What are the main philosophical ideas of realism?
6. Write a note on the influence of realism in education.
7. Describe the different Indian and western forms of realism.

References

1. Aggarwal, J.C. (2002). *Theory and Principles of Education*. New Delhi: Vikas Publishing House (P) Ltd.
2. Belock & Green J.L. (Ed.). *Philosophy and Education*. Meerut: Any Prakashan.
3. Bhattacharya, S. (1996). *Foundations of Education*. New Delhi: Atlantic Publishers and Distributors.
4. http://oregonstate.edu/instruct/ed416/PP2.html
5. http://the-difference-between.com/realism/pragmatism
6. http://www.jstor.org/stable/2012008?seq=1#page_scan_tab_contents
7. http://www.nordprag.org/papers/Kitcher5.pdf
8. http://www.slideshare.net/nikiduremdes/pragmatism-and-realism-presentation-831779
9. https://thewildwebster.wordpress.com/2012/02/02/pragmatism-vs-practical-realism/
10. https://www.cross-x.com/topic/9881-realism-vs-pragmatism/
11. https://www.quora.com/What-is-the-difference-between-Realism-and-Pragmatism
12. Ismail Thamarasseri & S. Sabu (2010) *Thoughts on Education*. New Delhi: Kanishka Publishers
13. Ismail Thamarasseri (2007) *Education in the Emerging Indian Society*. New Delhi: Kanishka Publishers

14. Kneller, G.F. (1971). *Introduction to the Philosophy of Education*. New York: John Willy and Sons.
15. Thamarasseri, I. (2014). *Philosophical Foundations of Education.* Agra: Shri Vinod Pustak Mandir

Chapter - 8

Socratic Method

Introduction

The **Socratic method**, also can be known as Socratic debate, is a form of **cooperative argumentative dialogue** between individuals, based on asking and answering questions to stimulate critical thinking and to draw out ideas and underlying presumptions. It is a **dialectical method**, involving a discussion in which the defence of one point of view is questioned; one participant may lead another to contradict themselves in some way, thus weakening the defender's point. This method is named after the Classical Greek philosopher Socrates and is introduced by him in Plato's *Theaetetus* as midwifery because it is employed to bring out definitions implicit in the interlocutors' beliefs, or to help them further their understanding.

The Socratic method is a method of hypothesis elimination, in that better hypotheses are found by steadily identifying and eliminating those that lead to contradictions. The Socratic method searches for general, commonly held truths that shape beliefs and scrutinizes them to determine their consistency with other beliefs. The basic form is a series of questions formulated as tests of logic and fact intended to help a person or group discover their beliefs about some topic, exploring definitions or logoi (singular logos) and seeking to characterize general characteristics shared by various particular instances.

In the second half of the 5th century BC, sophists were teachers who specialized in using the tools of philosophy and rhetoric to entertain, impress, or persuade an audience to accept the speaker's point of view. Socrates promoted an alternative method of teaching which came to be called the Socratic method.

Socrates began to engage in such discussions with his fellow **Athenians** after his friend from youth, **Chaerephon**, visited the **Oracle of Delphi**, which confirmed that no man in Greece was wiser than Socrates. Socrates saw this as a paradox, and began using the Socratic method to answer his conundrum. **Diogenes Laertius**, however, wrote that **Protagoras** invented the "Socratic" method.

Plato famously formalized the Socratic style in prose in some of his early dialogues, such as *Euthyphro* and *Ion*, and the method is most commonly found within the so-called "Socratic dialogues", which generally portray. Socrates engaging in the method and questioning his fellow citizens about moral and epistemological issues. But in his later dialogues, such as Theaetetus or Sophist, Plato had a different method to philosophical discussions, namely dialectic.

Method

Elenchus is the central technique of the Socratic method. The Latin form elenchus is used in English as the technical philosophical term. The most common adjectival form in English is **elenctic**. In Plato's early dialogues, the elenchus is the technique Socrates uses to investigate, for example, the nature or definition of ethical concepts such as justice or virtue. According to Vlastos, it has the following steps:

- Socrates' interlocutor asserts a thesis, for example "Courage is endurance of the soul", which Socrates considers false and targets for refutation.
- Socrates secures his interlocutor's agreement to further premises, for example "Courage is a fine thing" and "Ignorant endurance is not a fine thing".
- Socrates then argues, and the interlocutor agrees, that these further premises imply the contrary of the original

thesis; in this case, it leads to: "courage is not endurance of the soul".

- Socrates then claims that he has shown that his interlocutor's thesis is false and that its negation is true.

One elenctic examination can lead to a new, more refined, examination of the concept being considered, in this case it invites an examination of the claim: "Courage is wise endurance of the soul". Most Socratic inquiries consist of a series of elenchi and typically end in puzzlement known as aporia.

Frede points out that Vlastos' conclusion makes nonsense of the aporetic nature of the early dialogues. Having shown that a proposed thesis is false is insufficient to conclude that some other competing thesis must be true. Rather, the interlocutors have reached **aporia**, an improved state of still not knowing what to say about the subject under discussion.

The exact nature of the elenchus is subject to a great deal of debate, in particular concerning whether it is a positive method, leading to knowledge, or a negative method used solely to refute false claims to knowledge.

W. K. C. Guthrie in *The Greek Philosophers* sees it as an error to regard the Socratic method as a means by which one seeks the answer to a problem, or knowledge. Guthrie claims that the Socratic method actually aims to demonstrate one's ignorance. Socrates, unlike the Sophists, did believe that knowledge was possible, but believed that the first step to knowledge was recognition of one's ignorance. Guthrie writes, "[Socrates] was accustomed to say that he did not himself know anything, and that the only way in which he was wiser than other men was that he was conscious of his own ignorance, while they were not. The essence of the Socratic method is to convince the interlocutor that whereas he thought he knew something, in fact he does not."

Application

Socrates generally applied his method of examination to concepts that seem to lack any concrete definition; e.g., the key moral concepts at the time, the virtues of piety, wisdom, temperance, courage, and justice. Such an examination challenged the implicit moral beliefs of the interlocutors, bringing out inadequacies and inconsistencies in their beliefs, and usually resulting in aporia. In view of such inadequacies, Socrates himself professed his ignorance, but others still claimed to have knowledge. Socrates believed that his awareness of his ignorance made him wiser than those who, though ignorant, still claimed knowledge. While this belief seems paradoxical at first glance, it in fact allowed Socrates to discover his own errors where others might assume they were correct. This claim was known by the anecdote of the Delphic oracular pronouncement that Socrates was the wisest of all men.

Socrates used this claim of wisdom as the basis of his moral exhortation. Accordingly, he claimed that the chief goodness consists in the caring of the soul concerned with moral truth and moral understanding, that "wealth does not bring goodness, but goodness brings wealth and every other blessing, both to the individual and to the state", and that "life without examination is not worth living". It is with this in mind that the Socratic method is employed.

The motive for the modern usage of this method and Socrates' use are not necessarily equivalent. Socrates rarely used the method to actually develop consistent theories, instead using myth to explain them. The **Parmenides dialogue** shows Parmenides using the Socratic method to point out the flaws in the Platonic theory of the Forms, as presented by Socrates; it is not the only dialogue in which theories normally expounded by Plato/Socrates are broken down through dialectic. Instead of arriving at answers, the method was used to break down the theories we hold, to go "beyond" the axioms and postulates we take for granted. Therefore, myth and the Socratic method are not meant by Plato to be incompatible; they have different purposes, and are often described as the "left hand" and "right hand" paths to good and wisdom.

A **Socratic Circle** or **Socratic Seminar** is a pedagogical approach based on the Socratic method and uses a dialogic approach to understand information in a text. Its systematic procedure is used to examine a text through questions and answers founded on the beliefs that all new knowledge is connected to prior knowledge, that all thinking comes from asking questions, and that asking one question should lead to asking further questions. A Socratic Circle is not a debate. The goal of this activity is to have participants work together to construct meaning and arrive at an answer, not for one student or one group to "win the argument".

This approach is based on the belief that participants seek and gain deeper understanding of concepts in the text through thoughtful dialogue rather than memorizing information that has been provided for them. While **Socratic Circles** can differ in structure, and even in name, they typically involve the following components: a passage of text that students must read beforehand and two concentric circles of students: an outer circle and an inner circle. The inner circle focuses on exploring and analysing the text through the act of questioning and answering. During this phase, the outer circle remains silent. Students in the outer circle are much like scientific observers watching and listening to the conversation of the inner circle. When the text has been fully discussed and the inner circle is finished talking, the outer circle provides feedback on the dialogue that took place. This process alternates with the inner circle students going to the outer circle for the next meeting and vice versa. The length of this process varies depending on the text used for the discussion. The teacher may decide to alternate groups within one meeting, or they may alternate at each separate meeting.

The most significant difference between this activity and most typical classroom activities involves the role of the teacher. In Socratic Circles the students lead the discussion and questioning. The teacher's role is to ensure the discussion advances regardless of the particular direction the discussion takes.

Socratic Teaching

The oldest, and still the most powerful, teaching tactic for fostering critical thinking is **Socratic teaching**. In Socratic teaching we focus on giving students questions, not answers. We model an inquiring, probing mind by continually probing into the subject with questions. The abilities we gain by focusing on the elements of reasoning in a disciplined and self-assessing way, and the logical relationships that result from such disciplined thought, prepare us for Socratic questioning.

There is a predictable set of relationships that hold for all subjects and disciplines. This is given in the general logic of reasoning, since every subject has been developed by those who had:

- shared goals and objectives (which defined the subject focus)
- shared questions and problems (whose solution they pursued)
- shared information and data (which they used as an empirical basis)
- shared modes of interpreting or judging that information
- shared specialized concepts and ideas (which they used to help them organize their data)
- shared key assumptions (that gave them a basis from which to collectively begin)
- a shared point of view (which enabled them to pursue common goals from a common framework)

Each of the elements represents a dimension into which one can delve in questioning a person. We can question goals and purposes. We can probe into the nature of the question, problem, or issue that is on the floor. We can inquire into whether or not we have relevant data and information. We can consider alternative interpretations of the data and information. We can analyze key concepts and ideas. We can question assumptions being made. We can ask students to trace out the implications and consequences of what they are saying. We can consider alternative points of view. All of these, and more, are the proper focus of the Socratic questioner.

As a tactic and approach, Socratic questioning is a highly disciplined process. The Socratic questioner acts as the logical equivalent of the inner critical voice which the mind develops when it develops critical thinking abilities. The contributions from the members of the class are like so many thoughts in the mind. All of the thoughts must be dealt with and they must be dealt with carefully and fairly. By following up all answers with further questions, and by selecting questions which advance the discussion, the Socratic questioner forces the class to think in a disciplined, intellectually responsible manner, while yet continually aiding the students by posing facilitating questions. A Socratic questioner should:

- keep the discussion focused
- keep the discussion intellectually responsible
- stimulate the discussion with probing questions
- periodically summarize what has and what has not been dealt with and/or resolved
- draw as many students as possible into the discussion.

Lectures have their place in the world of education. We have all been in classes where the teacher did most of the talking. Sometimes this is a helpful way of taking in the information. Even watching video lessons is a little like listening to a lecture. The conversation is a one-way street, where you're listening and learning, and until you take the quiz, you do not necessarily get a chance to chime in with your own thoughts and knowledge.

The Socratic method is a different style of education than a lecture. This approach involves a conversation in which a student is asked to question their assumptions. It is a forum for open-ended inquiry, one in which both student and teacher can use probing questions to develop a deeper understanding of the topic.

Although it's unknown who first used this approach in history, the method is named for Socrates, an ancient Greek philosopher who was known for these types of conversations. Think of the Socratic method as mainly back and forth between a teacher, like Socrates, and a student. These types of conversations do not necessarily find all of the answers, but they raise new questions for consideration.

The Socratic method has sometimes been portrayed in movies or by particular teachers as an intimidating experience, where a teacher tries to put down the student's knowledge. However, the modern application of the method is mainly about gaining deeper understanding of a topic and not about condemning a student. The goal is greater knowledge, not just winning an argument or showing yourself to be superior.

How Does It Work?

The principle underlying the Socratic method is that students learn through the use of critical thinking, reasoning, and logic. This technique involves finding holes in their own theories and then patching them up. In law school specifically, a teacher will ask a series of Socratic questions after having a student summarize a case, including relevant legal principles associated with the case. Teachers often manipulate the facts or the legal principles associated with the case to demonstrate how the resolution of the case can change greatly if even one fact changes. The goal is for students to solidify their knowledge of the case by thinking critically under pressure.

This often rapid-fire exchange takes place in front of the entire class so students can practice thinking and making arguments on their feet. It also helps them master the art of speaking in front of large groups. Some law students find the process intimidating or humiliating but the Socratic method can actually produce a lively, engaging, and intellectual classroom atmosphere when it's done correctly by a great teacher.

Simply listening to a Socratic method discussion can help you even if you are not the student who is called on. Teachers use the Socratic method to keep students focused because the constant possibility of being called on in class causes students to closely follow the professor and the class discussion. It is important to remember that teachers are not using the Socratic seminar to embarrass students. It is a tool for mastering difficult concepts and principles. The Socratic method forces students to define, articulate and apply their thoughts. If the teacher gave all the answers and broke down the case himself, would you really be challenged?

When teachers use **Socratic questioning** in teaching, their purpose may be to probe student thinking, to determine the extent of student knowledge on a given topic, issue or subject, to model

Socratic questioning for students or to help students analyze a concept or line of reasoning. It is suggested that students should learn the discipline of Socratic questioning so that they begin to use it in reasoning through complex issues, in understanding and assessing the thinking of others and in following-out the implications of what they and others think. In fact, Socrates himself thought that questioning was the only defensible form of teaching.

In teaching, teachers can use Socratic questioning for at least two purposes: (1) To deeply probe student thinking, to help students begin to distinguish what they know or understand from what they do not know or understand and to help them develop intellectual humility in the process; (2) To foster students' abilities to ask Socratic questions, to help students acquire the powerful tools of Socratic dialogue, so that they can use these tools in everyday life and in questioning themselves and others. To this end, teachers can model the questioning strategies they want students to emulate and employ. Moreover, teachers need to directly teach students how to construct and ask deep questions. Beyond that, students need practice to improve their questioning abilities.

Socratic questioning illuminates the importance of questioning in learning. This includes differentiating between systematic and **fragmented thinking**, while forcing individuals to understand the root of their knowledge and ideas. Educators who support the use of Socratic Questioning in educational settings argues that it helps students become active and independent learners.

Summary

Socrates (470-399 BC) was a Greek philosopher who, despite being considered one of the greatest and most important philosophers who ever lived, left no writings at all. Most of what we know about his life and work comes from the writings of his disciples, **Xenophon** and **Plato**. He lived during a period of transition in the Greek empire, and after the **Peloponnesian War**, he was tried, convicted, and executed for corrupting the young. Socrates engaged in questioning of his students in an unending search for truth. He sought to get to the foundations of his students' and colleagues' views by asking continual questions until a contradiction was exposed, thus proving the fallacy of the initial assumption. This became known as the Socratic Method, and may be Socrates' most enduring contribution to philosophy. The Socratic method is a way to seek truths by your own lights. It is a system, a spirit, a method, a type of philosophical inquiry an intellectual technique, all rolled into one. Socrates himself never spelled out a "method." However, the Socratic method is named after him because Socrates, more than any other before or since, models for us philosophy practiced - philosophy as deed, as way of living, as something that any of us can do. It is an open system of **philosophical inquiry** that allows one to interrogate from many vantage points.

Model Questions

1. Write a short note on Socratic Method.
2. Briefly narrate the origin and development of Socratic Method.
3. Narrate the ideas of Socratics on Socratic Methodologies.
4. Distinguish between Socratic method and Question-Answer method.
5. How Socratic method and lecture method differ?
6. What are the precautions a need to be taken by a Socratic questioner?

References

1. Areeda, Philip E. 'The Socratic Method' (1996) 109(5) Harvard Law Review 911-922
2. Benson, Hugh (2000) Socratic Wisdom. Oxford: Oxford University Press.
3. Books
4. Darvhisi, Dariush, "Distinction between Dialectical methods of Socrates and Plato", Logical Study, Volume & Issue: Volume 2, Number 4, Winter 2012, pp. 49–76.
5. Frede, Michael (1992) 'Plato's Arguments and the Dialogue Form' in Oxford Studies in Ancient Philosophy, Supplementary Volume, 201-19.
6. Gregory Vlastos, 'The Socratic Elenchus', Oxford Studies in Ancient Philosophy I, Oxford 1983, 27–58.
7. Guthrie, W. K. C. (1968) The Greek Philosophers from Thales to Aristotle. London: Routledge.
8. http://www.criticalthinking.org/pages/socratic-teaching/606
9. http://www.garlikov.com/Soc_Meth.html
10. http://www.philosopher.org/Socratic_Method.html

11. https://education.cu-portland.edu/blog/classroom-resources/should-educators-use-the-socratic-method-of-teaching/
12. https://en.wikipedia.org/wiki/Socratic_method
13. https://en.wikipedia.org/wiki/Socratic_questioning
14. https://study.com/academy/lesson/what-is-the-socratic-method-definition-examples.html
15. https://www.law.uchicago.edu/socratic-method
16. https://www.merriam-webster.com/dictionary/Socratic%20method
17. https://www.thoughtco.com/what-is-the-socratic-method-2154875
18. https://www.youtube.com/watch?v=_CPLu3qCbSU
19. https://www.youtube.com/watch?v=EB4MYGlnRl4
20. https://www.youtube.com/watch?v=tw45yU6yh-E
21. Jarratt, Susan C. (1991) Rereading the Sophists: Classical Rhetoric Refigured. Carbondale and Edwardsville: Southern Illinois University Press.
22. Jarratt, Susan C. Rereading the Sophists: Classical Rhetoric Refigured. Carbondale and Edwardsville: Southern Illinois University Press, 1991., p. 83.
23. Liddell, Scott and Jones, Greek-English Lexicon, 9th Edition.
24. Michael Frede, "Plato's Arguments and the Dialogue Form", Oxford Studies in Ancient Philosophy, Supplementary Volume 1992, Oxford 1992, 201–19.
25. Sprague, Rosamond Kent (1972) The Older Sophists. Indianapolis: Hackett Publishing Company
26. Sprague, Rosamond Kent, The Older Sophists, Hackett Publishing Company (ISBN 0-87220-556-8), p. 5.
27. Stephen Salkever, "Methods of Interpreting Plato and his Dialogues" (Bryn Mawr Classical Review)
28. Vlastos, Gregory; Vlastos (1983). "The Socratic Elenchus". Oxford Studies in Ancient Philosophy. 1: 27–58.
29. Webster's New World College Dictionary, 4th Edition; Oxford English Dictionary.

Chapter - 9

Pythagoras

Life

Pythagoras was born in 570 BC at Samos, Ionia of Greece and died on 500-490 BC at Metapontum, Lucanium of Italy. His father, Mnesarchus, was a gem merchant. His mother's name was Pythais. Pythagoras had two or three brothers. Some historians say that Pythagoras was married to a woman named Theano and had a daughter Damo, and a son named Telauges, who succeeded Pythagoras as a teacher and possibly taught Empedocles. Others say that Theano was one of his students, not his wife, and say that Pythagoras never married and had no children. Pythagoras was an Greek philosopher, mathematician, and founder of the Pythagorean brotherhood that, although religious in nature, formulated principles that influenced the thought of **Plato** and **Aristotle** and contributed to the development of mathematics and Western rational philosophy.

Pythagoras emigrated to southern Italy about 532 BC, apparently to escape Samos's tyrannical rule, and established his ethico-political academy at Croton (now Crotone, Italy). It is difficult to distinguish Pythagoras's teachings from those of his disciples. None of his writings have survived, and Pythagoreans invariably supported their doctrines by indiscriminately citing their master's authority. Pythagoras, however, is generally credited with the theory of the functional significance of **numbers** in the **objective world** and in **music**. Other discoveries often attributed to him were probably developed only later by the Pythagorean school. More probably, the bulk of the intellectual tradition originating with Pythagoras himself belongs to mystical wisdom rather than to scientific scholarship.

Teachings

Pythagoras is often referred to as the first pure mathematician. Pythagoras was well educated, and he played the lyre throughout his lifetime, knew poetry and recited Homer. He was interested in mathematics, philosophy, astronomy and music, and was greatly influenced by **Pherekydes** (philosophy), **Thales** (mathematics and astronomy) and **Anaximander** (philosophy, geometry). Pythagoras left Samos for Egypt in about 535 B.C. to study with the priests in the temples. Many of the practices of the society he created later in Italy can be traced to the beliefs of Egyptian priests, such as the codes of secrecy, striving for purity, and refusal to eat beans or to wear animal skins as clothing. Ten years later, when **Persia** invaded Egypt, Pythagoras was taken prisoner and sent to Babylon (now Iraq), where he met the Magoi, priests who taught him sacred rites. **Iamblichus** (250-330 AD), a Syrian philosopher, wrote about Pythagoras, "He also reached the acme of perfection in arithmetic and music and the other mathematical sciences taught by the Babylonians"

In 520 BC, Pythagoras, now a free man, left Babylon and returned to **Samos**, and sometime later began a school called The **Semicircle**. His methods of teaching were not popular with the leaders of Samos, and their desire for him to become involved in politics did not appeal to him, so he left. Pythagoras settled in **Crotona**, a Greek colony in southern Italy, about 518 BC, and founded a philosophical and religious school where his many followers lived and worked. The Pythagoreans lived by rules of behaviour, including when they spoke, what they wore and what they ate. Pythagoras was the Master of the society, and the followers, both men and women, who also lived there, were known as **mathematikoi**. They had no personal possessions and were vegetarians. Another group of followers who lived apart from the school were allowed to have personal possessions and were not expected to be vegetarians.

They all worked communally on discoveries and theories. Pythagoras believed: All things are numbers. **Mathematics** is the basis for everything, and **geometry** is the highest form of mathematical studies. The physical world can understood through mathematics. The soul resides in the brain, and is immortal. It moves from one being to another, sometimes from a human into an animal, through a series of reincarnations called transmigration until it becomes pure. Pythagoras believed that both mathematics and music could purify. Numbers have personalities, characteristics, strengths and weaknesses. The world depends upon the interaction of opposites, such as male and female, lightness and darkness, warm and cold, dry and moist, light and heavy, fast and slow. Certain symbols have a mystical significance. All members of the society should observe strict loyalty and secrecy. Because of the strict secrecy among the members of Pythagoras' society, and the fact that they shared ideas and intellectual discoveries within the group and did not give individuals credit, it is difficult to be certain whether all the theorems attributed to Pythagoras were originally his, or whether they came from the communal society of the Pythagoreans.

Some of the students of Pythagoras eventually wrote down the theories, teachings and discoveries of the group, but the Pythagoreans always gave credit to Pythagoras as the Master for: The sum of the angles of a triangle is equal to two right angles. The theorem of Pythagoras - for a right-angled triangle the square on the hypotenuse is equal to the sum of the squares on the other two sides. The Babylonians understood this 1000 years earlier, but Pythagoras proved it. Constructing figures of a given area and geometrical algebra. For example they solved various equations by geometrical means. The discovery of irrational numbers is attributed to the Pythagoreans, but seems unlikely to have been the idea of Pythagoras because it does not align with his philosophy the all things are numbers, since number to him meant the ratio of two whole numbers.

The **five regular solids** are tetrahedron, cube, octahedron, icosahedron, dodecahedron. It is believed that Pythagoras knew how to construct the first three but not last two. Pythagoras taught that

Earth was a sphere in the centre of the **Cosmos** (Universe), that the planets, stars, and the universe were spherical because the sphere was the most perfect solid figure. He also taught that the paths of the planets were circular. Pythagoras recognized that the morning star was the same as the evening star, **Venus**.

Pythagoras studied odd and even numbers, triangular numbers, and perfect numbers. Pythagoreans contributed to our understanding of angles, triangles, areas, proportion, polygons, and polyhedra. Pythagoras also related music to mathematics. He had long played the seven string lyre, and learned how harmonious the vibrating strings sounded when the lengths of the strings were proportional to whole numbers, such as 2:1, 3:2, 4:3. Pythagoreans also realized that this knowledge could be applied to other musical instruments. The Pythagorean Theorem is a cornerstone of mathematics, and continues to be so interesting to mathematicians that there are more than 400 different proofs of the theorem. Pythagoras wanted to improve the music of his day, which he believed was not harmonious enough and was too hectic. According to legend, he discovered that musical notes could be translated into mathematical equations by listening to blacksmiths at work. "Pythagorean tuning" is a system of musical tuning in which the frequency relationships of all intervals are based on the ratio 3:2 (a stack of perfect fifths), a system which has been documented as long ago as 3500 B.C. in Babylonian texts, but which is nevertheless often attributed to Pythagoras. He also believed in the "musica universalis" (or the "harmony of the spheres"), the idea that the planets and stars moved according to mathematical equations, which corresponded to musical notes and thus produced a kind of symphony.

Central Beliefs

The school that Pythagoras established at **Croton** was in some ways more of a secret brotherhood or **monastery**. It was based on his religious teachings and was highly concerned with the morality of society. Members were required to live ethically, love one another, share political beliefs, practice pacifism, and devote themselves to the mathematics of nature. They also abstained from meat, abjured personal property and observed a rule of silence (called "echemythia"), the breaking of which was punishable by death, based on the belief that if someone was in any doubt as to what to say, they should remain silent.

Pythagoras saw his religious and scientific views as inseparably interconnected. He believed in the theory of **metempsychosis** or the **transmigration** of the soul and its **reincarnation** again and again after death into the bodies of humans, animals or vegetables until it became moral. He was one of the first to propose that the thought processes and the soul were located in the brain and not the heart.

Another of Pythagoras' central beliefs was that the **essence of being** can be found in the form of numbers, and that it can be encountered through the study of mathematics. For instance, he believed that things like health relied on a stable proportion of elements, with too much or too little of one thing causing an imbalance that makes a person unhealthy. In mathematics, Pythagoras is commonly given credit for discovering what is now know as the **Pythagorean Theorem**, a theorem in geometry that states that, in a right-angled triangle, the square of the hypotenuse is equal to the sum of the squares of the other two sides. Although this had been known and utilized previously by the **Babylonians** and Indians, he is thought to have constructed the first proof.

Pythagoras believed that the **number system** and the **universe system** was based on the sum of the numbers one to four, and that odd numbers were masculine and even numbers were feminine. He discovered the theory of mathematical proportions, constructed from three to five geometrical solids, and also discovered square numbers and square roots. The discovery of the golden ratio is also usually attributed to Pythagoras, or possibly to his student, **Theano**.

Pythagoras was one of the first to think that the **Earth** was round, that all planets have an **axis**, and that all the planets travel around one central point. He also believed that the **Moon** was another planet that he called a "counter-Earth".

Any responsible account of Pythagoras' philosophy must be based in the first place on the evidence prior to Aristotle and in the second place on evidence that our sources explicitly identify as deriving from Aristotle's books on the Pythagoreans as well as from the books of his pupils such as **Aristoxenus** and **Dicaearchus**. There is general agreement as to what the pre-Aristotelian evidence is, although there are differences in interpretation of it. There is less agreement as to what should be included in Aristotle's, Dicaearchus' and Aristoxenus' evidence. In the face of the Pythagorean question and the problems that arise even regarding the early sources, it is reasonable to wonder if we can say anything about Pythagoras. A minimalist might argue that the early evidence only allows us to conclude that Pythagoras was a historical figure who achieved fame for his wisdom but that it is impossible to determine in what that wisdom consisted. We might say that he was interested in the fate of the soul and taught a way of life, but we can say nothing precise about the nature of that life or what he taught about the soul. There is some reason to believe, however, that something more than this can be said.

The Philosophy of Pythagoras

Pythagoras argued that there are three kinds of men, just as there are three classes of strangers who come to the Olympic Games. The lowest consists of those who come to buy and sell, and next above them are those who come to compete. Best of all are those who simply come to look on. Men may be classified accordingly as **lovers of wisdom**, **lovers of honour**, and **lovers of gain**. That seems to imply the doctrine of the tripartite soul, which is also attributed to the early Pythagoreans on good authority, though it is common now to ascribe it to Plato. There are, however, clear references to it before his time, and it agrees much better with the general outlook of the **Pythagoreans**. The comparison of human life to a gathering like the Games was often repeated in later days. Pythagoras also taught the **Doctrine of Rebirth** or **transmigration**, which we may have learned from the contemporary **Orphics**. **Xenophanes** made fun of him for pretending to recognize the voice of a departed friend in the howls of a beaten dog. **Empedocles** seems to be referring to him when he speaks of a man who could remember what happened ten or twenty generations before. It was on this that the doctrine of Recollection, which plays so great a part in Plato, was based.

The things we perceive with the senses, Plato argues, remind us of things we knew when the soul was out of the body and could perceive reality directly.

There is more difficulty about the cosmology of Pythagoras. Hardly any school ever professed such reverence for its founder's authority as the Pythagoreans. 'The Master said so' was their watchword. On the other hand, few schools have shown so much capacity for progress and for adapting themselves to new conditions. Pythagoras started from the cosmical system of **Anaximenes**. Aristotle tells us that the Pythagoreans represented the world as inhaling 'air' form the boundless mass outside it, and this 'air' is identified with 'the unlimited'. When, however, we come to the process by which things are developed out of the 'unlimited', we observe a great change. We hear nothing more of 'separating out' or even of rarefaction and condensation. Instead of that we have the theory that what gives form to the Unlimited is the Limit. That is the great contribution of Pythagoras to philosophy, and we must try to understand it. Now the function of the Limit is usually illustrated from the arts of music and medicine, and we have seen how important these two arts were for Pythagoreans, so it is natural to infer that the key to its meaning is to be found in them.

It may be taken as certain that Pythagoras himself discovered the numerical ratios which determine the concordant intervals of the musical scale. Similar to musical intervals, in medicine there are opposites, such as the hot and the cold, the wet and the dry, and it is the business of the physician to produce a proper 'blend' of these in the human body. In a well-known passage of **Plato's Phaedo** we are told by **Simmias** that the Pythagoreans held the body to be strung like an instrument to a certain pitch, hot and cold, wet and dry taking the place of high and low in music. Musical tuning and health are alike means arising from the application of Limit to the Unlimited. It was natural for Pythagoras to look for something of the same kind in the world at large. Briefly stated, the doctrine of Pythagoras was that all things are numbers. In certain fundamental cases, the early Pythagoreans represented numbers and explained their properties by means of dots arranged in certain 'figures' or patterns.

Was Pythagoras A Mathematician or Cosmologist?

In the modern world Pythagoras is most of all famous as a mathematician, because of the theorem named after him, and secondarily as a cosmologist, because of the striking view of a universe ascribed to him in the later tradition, in which the heavenly bodies produce "the music of the spheres" by their movements. Neither **Plato** nor **Aristotle** treats Pythagoras as having contributed to the development of Presocratic cosmology, although Aristotle in particular discusses the topic in some detail in the first book of the **Metaphysics** and elsewhere. Aristotle evidently knows of no cosmology of Pythagoras that antedates the cosmological system of the "so-called Pythagoreans," which he dates to the middle of the fifth century, and which is found in the fragments of **Philolaus**. There is also no mention of Pythagoras' work in geometry or of the Pythagorean theorem in the early evidence. **Dicaearchus** comments that "what he said to his associates no one can say reliably," but then identifies four doctrines that became well known: 1) that the soul is immortal; 2) that it transmigrates into other kinds of animals; 3) that after certain intervals the things that have happened once happen again, so that nothing is completely new; 4) that all animate beings belong to the same family. Thus, for Dicaearchus too, it is not as a mathematician or Presocratic writer on nature that Pythagoras is famous. It might not be too surprising that Plato, Aristotle and Dicaearchus do not mention Pythagoras' work in mathematics, because they are not primarily dealing with the history of mathematics. On the other hand, Aristotle's pupil **Eudemus** did write a history of geometry in the fourth century and what we find in Eudemus is very significant. **Eudemus** is reported as beginning with **Thales** and an obscure figure named **Mamercus**, but the third person mentioned by Proclus in this report is Pythagoras, immediately before Anaxagoras. Even those who want to assign Pythagoras a larger role in early Greek mathematics recognize that most of what Proclus says here cannot go back to **Eudemus**. Thus, not only is Pythagoras not commonly known as a geometer in the time of Plato and Aristotle, but also the most authoritative history of early Greek geometry assigns him no role in the history of geometry in the overview preserved in Proclus. According to Proclus, Eudemus did report that two propositions, which are later found in Euclid's Elements, were discoveries of the Pythagoreans. Eudemus does not assign the discoveries to any specific Pythagorean, and they are hard to date. The discoveries might be as early as **Hippasus** in the middle of the fifth century, who is associated with a group of Pythagoreans known as the **mathematici**, who arose after Pythagoras' death. The crucial point to note is that Eudemus does not assign these discoveries to Pythagoras himself. The first Pythagorean whom we can confidently identify as an accomplished mathematician is Archytas in the late fifth and the first half of the fourth century.

Summary

The pre-Socratic Greek philosopher **Pythagoras** must have been one of the world's greatest persons. It is also hard to say how much of what we are told about the life of Pythagoras is trustworthy; for a mass of legend gathered around his name at an early date. Sometimes he is represented as a man of science, and sometimes as a preacher of mystic doctrines, and we might be tempted to regard one or other of those characters as alone historical. The union of mathematical genius and mysticism is common enough. Originally from Samos, Pythagoras founded at Kroton (in southern Italy) a society which was at once a religious community and a scientific school. It is stated that Pythagoras was a disciple of **Anaximander**, his astronomy was the natural development of Anaximander's. Also, the way in which the Pythagorean geometry developed also bears witness to its descent from that of **Miletos**. The great problem at this date was the duplication of the square, a problem which gave rise to the theorem of the square on the hypotenuse, commonly known still as the Pythagorean proposition.

Model Questions

1. Explain the Philosophy of Pythagoras.
2. Briefly narrate the life sketch of Pythagoras.
3. Distinguish the ideas of Pythagoras with anyone of contemporary philosophers.
4. Narrate the Mathematical elements of Pythagoras's philosophy?

5. Critically analyse the Pythagoras's thoughts on music.
6. How Pythagoras perceiving human knowledge and wisdom?

References

1. B L van der Waerden, Science Awakening (New York, 1954).
2. C J de Vogel, Pythagoras and Early Pythagoreanism (1966).
3. D J O'Meara, Pythagoras revived : Mathematics and philosophy in late antiquity (New York, 1990).
4. Diogenes Laertius, Lives of eminent philosophers (New York, 1925).
5. E S Stamatis, Pythagoras of Samos (Greek) (Athens, 1981).
6. H Wussing, Pythagoras, in H Wussing and W Arnold, Biographien bedeutender Mathematiker (Berlin, 1983).
7. http://www.philosimply.com/philosopher/pythagoras
8. http://www.storyofmathematics.com/greek_pythagoras.html
9. http://www-groups.dcs.st-and.ac.uk/history/Biographies/Pythagoras.html
10. https://en.oxforddictionaries.com/definition/pythagoras
11. https://en.wikipedia.org/wiki/Pythagoras
12. https://en.wikiquote.org/wiki/Pythagoras
13. https://plato.stanford.edu/entries/pythagoras/
14. https://www.britannica.com/biography/Pythagoras
15. https://www.iep.utm.edu/pythagor/
16. https://www.mathopenref.com/pythagoras.html
17. https://www.philosophybasics.com/philosophers_pythagoras.html
18. https://www.youtube.com/watch?v=RsCzG-gsnPw
19. I Levy, La légende de Pythagore de Grèce en Ralestine (Paris, 1927).
20. Iamblichus, Life of Pythagoras (translated into English by T Taylor) (London, 1818).
21. L E Navia, Pythagoras : An annotated bibliography (New York, 1990).
22. L Ya Zhmud', Pythagoras and his school (Russian), From the History of the World Culture 'Nauka' (Leningrad, 1990).
23. M Cerchez, Pythagoras (Romanian) (Bucharest, 1986).
24. P Gorman, Pythagoras, a life (1979).
25. Porphyry, Life of Pythagoras in M Hadas and M Smith, Heroes and Gods (London, 1965)..
26. Porphyry, Vita Pythagorae (Leipzig, 1886),
27. R S Brumbaugh, The philosophers of Greece (Albany, N.Y., 1981).
28. T L Heath, A history of Greek mathematics 1 (Oxford, 1931).

Chapter - 10

Heraclitus

Life

Heraclitus of Ephesus (c. 535 - 475 B.C.) was a Pre-Socratic Greek philosopher from Ephesus, on the Ionian coast of modern-day **Turkey**. He is sometimes mentioned in connection with the Ephesian School of philosophy, although he was really the only prominent member of that school. He was the first Western philosopher to go beyond physical theory in search of metaphysical foundations and moral applications, and some consider him, along with Parmenides, the most significant of the Pre-Socratic philosophers. His idea of a universe in constant change but with an underlying **order or reason** (which he called **Logos**) forms the essential foundation of the European worldview. Many subsequent philosophers, from Plato to Aristotle, from the Stoics to the Church Fathers, from Georg Hegel to Alfred North Whitehead, have claimed to have been influenced by the ideas of Heraclitus.

According to the 3rd Century historian **Diogenes Laertius**, Heraclitus flourished in the 69th Olympiad, but the dates of his birth and death are just guesswork based on that. So, all we can say it is it is likely that he was born around 535 B.C. We do know that he was born to an aristocratic family in **Ephesus**, an important city on the Ionian coast of modern-day Turkey.

His father was named either Bloson, and was a powerful figure in the city. But, according to Diogenes Laertius, Heraclitus abdicated the kingship in favour of his brother, and had no interest in politics or power. As a youth, he was a prodigious intellect, and he claimed to have taught himself everything he knew by a process of self-questioning. Some sources also say that he was a pupil of Xenophanes (570 - 480 B.C.)

He was sometimes known as "**the Obscure**" (or "**the Dark**") for the deliberate difficulty and unclearness of his teachings. He was also known as the "Weeping Philosopher", and it is speculated that he was prone to melancholia or depression, which prevented him from finishing some of his works. There is no record of his having travelled, even as far as the nearby learning centre of **Miletus**, although he seems to have been familiar with the ideas of the **Milesian School**.

He was apparently something of a misanthrope and a loner, and he cultivated an aristocratic disdain for the masses and favoured the rule of a few wise men. He was not afraid to scorn and denigrate almost everyone from the Ephesians to the Athenians to the Persian leader, Darius. He believed that the poet Hesiod and Pythagoras "lacked understanding", and claimed that Homer and Archilochus deserved to be beaten. Diogenes Laertius reported that, later in life, he wandered the mountains, eating only grass and herbs. His years of wandering in the wilderness, resulted in an oedema (dropsy) and impairment of vision. After 24 hours of his own idiosyncratic treatment, he died and was interred in the marketplace of Ephesus.

Theory of Knowledge

Heraclitus sees the great majority of human beings as lacking understanding. Of this Word's being forever do men prove to be uncomprehending, both before they hear and once they have heard it. For although all things happen according to this Word they are like the unexperienced experiencing words and deeds. Other men are unaware of what they do when they are awake just as they are forgetful of what they do when they are asleep.

Most people sleep-walk through life, not understanding what is going on about them. Yet experience of words and deeds can enlighten those who are receptive to their meaning. On the one hand,

Heraclitus commends **sense experience**: "The things of which there is sight, hearing, experience, I prefer". On the other hand, "Poor witnesses for men are their eyes and ears if they have barbarian souls". A barbarian is one who does not speak the Greek language. Thus while sense experience seems necessary for understanding, if we do not know the right language, we cannot interpret the information the senses provide. Heraclitus does not give a detailed and systematic account of the respective roles of experience and reason in knowledge. But we can learn something from his manner of expression.

Describing the practice of religious prophets, Heraclitus says, "The Lord whose oracle is at Delphi neither reveals nor conceals, but gives a sign". Similarly, Heraclitus does not reveal or conceal, but produces complex expressions that have encoded in them multiple messages for those who can interpret them. He uses puns, paradoxes, antitheses, parallels, and various rhetorical and literary devices to construct expressions that have meanings beyond the obvious. This practice, together with his emphasis on the **Word (Logos)** as an ordering principle of the world, suggests that he sees his own expressions as imitations of the world with its structural and semantic complexity. To read Heraclitus the reader must solve verbal puzzles, and to learn to solve these puzzles is to learn to read the signs of the world. Heraclitus stresses the inductive rather than the deductive method of grasping the world, a world that is rationally structured, if we can but discern its shape.

For those who can discern it, the Word has an overriding message to impart: "Listening not to me but to the Word it is wise to agree that all things are one". It is perhaps Heraclitus's chief project to explain in what sense all things are one.

The Doctrine of Flux and the Unity of Opposites

According to both **Plato** and **Aristotle**, Heraclitus held extreme views that led to logical incoherence. For he held that (1) everything is constantly changing and (2) opposite things are identical, so that (3) everything is and is not at the same time. In other words, Universal Flux and the Identity of Opposites entail a denial of the

Law of Non-Contradiction. Plato indicates the source of the flux doctrine: "Heraclitus, I believe, says that all things go and nothing stays, and comparing existents to the flow of a river, he says you could not step twice into the same river".

What Heraclitus actually says is the following: "On those stepping into rivers staying the same other and other waters flow. There is an **antithesis** between 'same' and 'other.' The sentence says that different waters flow in rivers staying the same. In other words, though the waters are always changing, the rivers stay the same. Indeed, it must be precisely because the waters are always changing that there are rivers at all, rather than lakes or ponds. The message is that rivers can stay the same over time even though, or indeed because, the waters change. The point, then, is not that everything is changing, but that the fact that some things change makes possible the continued existence of other things. Perhaps more generally, the change in elements or constituents supports the constancy of higher-level structures. As for the alleged **doctrine of the Identity of Opposites**, Heraclitus does believe in some kind of unity of opposites. For instance, "God is day night, winter summer, war peace, satiety hunger". But if we look closer, we see that the unity in question is not identity: "As the same thing in us is living and dead, waking and sleeping, young and old. For these things having changed around are those, and conversely those having changed around are these".

And Heraclitus insists on the common-sense truth of change: "Cold things warm up, the hot cools off, wet becomes dry, dry becomes wet". This sort of mutual change presupposes the non-identity of the terms. What Heraclitus wishes to maintain is not the identity of opposites but the fact that they replace each other in a series of transformations: they are interchangeable or transformationally equivalent.

Thus, Heraclitus does not hold **Universal Flux**, but recognizes a law-like flux of elements; and he does not hold the **Identity of Opposites**, but the **Transformational Equivalence** of Opposites. The views that he does hold do not, jointly or separately, entail a denial of the Law of Non-Contradiction. Heraclitus does, to be sure, make paradoxical statements, but his views are no more self-contradictory than are the paradoxical claims of Socrates. They are, presumably, meant to wake us up from our dogmatic slumbers.

Knowledge

Plato held that for Heraclitus knowledge is made impossible by the flux of **sensible objects**. Yet Heraclitus does not repudiate knowledge or the wisdom that comes from a proper understanding of the world. To be sure, he believes most people are not capable of wisdom; understanding is a rare and precious commodity, which even most reputed sages do not attain to. Yet wisdom is possible, and it is embodied in Heraclitus' message, for those who can discern it.

Heraclitus seems to accept the evidence of the senses as in some way valuable: "The things of which there is sight, hearing, experience, I prefer". Sight is the best of the senses: "The eyes are more accurate witnesses than the ears". Yet in contrast to those who view knowledge as an accumulation of information or wisdom as a collection of sayings, he requires much more than **sensation** and memory: "Learning many things does not teach understanding. Else it would have taught **Hesiod** and **Pythagoras**, as well as **Xenophanes**".

In this statement Heraclitus reviews the leading authorities of his day, dealing with religious and secular knowledge, and finds them all wanting. They spend too much effort in collecting information and not enough in grasping its meaning. "What intelligence or understanding do the people have?" asks Heraclitus. "They follow popular bards and treat the crowd as their instructor, not realizing that the many are base, while the few are noble". He criticizes Hesiod on specifics: "The teacher of the multitude is Hesiod; they believe he has the greatest knowledge–who did not comprehend day and night: for they are one". In his myths, Hesiod treats Day and Night as separate persons, taking turns travelling abroad, while one remains at home. But this fails to capture the interconnectedness of day and night, and falsifies reality. Heraclitus criticizes **Homer**, **Pythagoras** and **Archilochus** for their inadequacies.

In general, Heraclitus holds that people do not learn what they should: "Many do not understand such things as they encounter, nor do they learn by their experience, but they think they do". Indeed, they do not process the information they receive: "Having heard without comprehension they are like the deaf; this saying bears witness to them: present they are absent". Heraclitus explains: "Poor witnesses for men are the eyes and ears of those who have barbarian souls". Most people perceive without understanding the world around them. **Sense perception** is necessary for knowledge, but not sufficient; without the ability to decipher information from the senses, one cannot understand the world.

What chance is there then to learn the secrets of the world? Heraclitus is not wholly pessimistic about human cognitive abilities: "All men have a share in self-knowledge and sound thinking". What is needed is not simply more sense experience or more information, but an improved way of comprehending the message (logos) that the world offers. In this context his curious method of expression begins to make sense. He presents his statements in the form of puzzles, riddles, apercus. Many of them support two or more readings, and contain hidden insights. To comprehend them the reader must grasp their complexity and then discover their unity. To read Heraclitus appropriately is to have a rich cognitive experience, as the philosopher hints in his introduction.

Heraclitus often presents a simple concrete situation or image which has implications for our understanding of the world: a river, a bow, a road. He does not generally pronounce generalizations and deduce consequences. Rather, his method can be seen as **inductive**: he offers an example which suggests general principles. Unlike most philosophers, he challenges the right brain rather than the left. He does not teach in the conventional sense; he offers his readers materials for understanding and lets them educate themselves. He cites with approval a model of religious instruction.

Ontology

The standard view of Heraclitus' ontology since Aristotle is that he is a material monist who holds that fire is the ultimate reality; all things are just manifestations of fire. According to Aristotle the **Milesians** in general were material **monists** who advocated other kinds of ultimate matter: Thales - water, Anaximander - the boundless, Anaximenes - air. So Heraclitus' theory was just another version of a common background theory. There are problems already with Aristotle's understanding of the Milesians: Aristotle lacks any textual evidence for Thales' view and must reconstruct it out of almost nothing; he sometimes treats Anaximander as a pluralist like **Anaxagoras** who thinks the boundless is a mixture of qualities; at most Anaximenes might exemplify **material monism**–but Plato reads him as a pluralist. In the case of Heraclitus, his own statements make material monism problematic as an interpretation.

According to **material monism**, some kind of matter is the ultimate reality, and any variation in the world consists merely of qualitative or possibly quantitative change in it; for there is only one reality, for instance fire, which can never come into existence or perish, but can only change in its appearances. Heraclitus, however, advocates a radical kind of change: "For souls it is death to become water, for water death to become earth, but from earth water is born, and from water soul".

The language of birth and death in the world of living things is precisely the language used in Greek metaphysics for coming to be and perishing. It implies a radical transformation that rules out continuing identity. Indeed, interpreters of Heraclitus cannot have it both ways: Heraclitus cannot be both a believer in **radical flux** and an advocate of monism. Either he must believe in a merely illusory or at most a limited kind of change, or he must be a pluralist.

One further difficulty remains for the monist reading. In Heraclitus's alleged version of monism, fire is the ultimate reality. Yet **fire** is the least substantial and the most evanescent of elemental stuffs. It makes a better **symbol of change** than of permanence. Other alleged cases of material monism offer a basic kind of matter that could arguably be stable and permanent over long periods of time; but fire manifests "need and satiety", a kind of ongoing consumption that can live only by devouring fuel. Is not Heraclitus' choice of a basic reality itself paradoxical? At best his appeal to fire seems to draw on material monism in a way that points beyond the theory to an account in which the process of change is more real than the material substances that undergo change.

Cosmology

Although Heraclitus is more than a **cosmologist**, he does offer a cosmology. His most fundamental statement on cosmology is found is: "This world-order [kosmos], the same of all, no god nor man did create, but it ever was and is and will be: ever living fire, kindling in measures and being quenched in measures". In this passage, he uses, for the first time in any extant Greek text, the word kosmos "order" to mean something like "world." He identifies the world with fire, but goes on to specify portions of fire that are kindling and being quenched. Although ancient sources, including Aristotle as well as the Stoics, attributed to Heraclitus a world that was periodically destroyed by fire and then reborn, the present statement seems to contradict that view, as Hegel already noticed. If the world always was and is and will be, then it does not perish and come back into existence, though portions of it are constantly being transformed.

Heraclitus describes the transformations of elementary bodies: The turnings of fire: first sea, and of sea half is earth, half **fire-burst**. Earth is liquefied as sea and measured into the same proportion as it had before it became earth. Fire turns into water / sea, and then half of that quantity turns into earth and half into "fireburst". The portion that becomes earth turns back into water, in the same quantity it had previously. Here Heraclitus envisages a law like transformation of stuff from fire to water to earth; the transformation is reversible, and in it the same relative quantities of stuff are preserved. There is, then, a kind of conservation of matter, or at least overall quantity of matter. What would make the world to be continuous would be the fact that when one portion of fire turns into water, an equivalent portion of water turns into fire. The overall equilibrium is preserved, even if the water that is now in the sea is not the same water as was in it before. This picture bears a similarity to the image of the river, which remains the same despite its changing material contents.

In this view of the world, the mutual transformations of matter are not an accidental feature, but the very essence of nature. Without change, there would be no world. Heraclitus seems to acknowledge this in his **praise of war** and strife: We must recognize that war is common, strife is justice, and all things happen according to strife and necessity. War is father of all and king of all; and some he manifested as gods, some as men; some he made slaves, some free.

Conflicting powers of opposites, including those of elemental bodies, make possible the world and all its variety; without that conflict we would have only lifeless uniformity. Heraclitus provided some sort of discussion of **meteorological and astronomical phenomena**. He studied the disappearance and reappearance of the moon at the end and beginning of a month. It is the clearest evidence that Heraclitus had a scientific interest in **astronomy**. He explained the sun and moon as bowls full of fire. As the moon's bowl rotated it caused the phases. **Eclipses** were the result of a rotation of the convex side of the bowls to face the earth. We have no reports about the earth itself, but we may suppose that, like his predecessors, Heraclitus viewed it as flat. Evaporations from the earth and sea apparently provided fuel for the heavenly bodies, which burned like oil lamps.

Divine power is manifest in all phenomena: "God is day night, winter summer, war peace, satiety hunger, and he alters just as fire when it is mixed with spices is named according to the aroma of each of them". Again Heraclitus seems to stress the unity of divine power, even if humans assign different names and attributes to it. All things that happen are good, but humans do not perceive them to be so: "To God all things are fair, good and just, but men suppose some things are unjust, some just". Heraclitus does not attempt to provide a detailed theodicy, but seeks to view all things sub specie, in which conflict keeps the world going.

Summary

Heraclitus was an ancient greek philosopher born in Ephesus. Heraclitus famously wrote in a way that is very hard to read, and for that reason the other philosopher's called him **"The Obscure"** and **"The Riddler."** He believed there was a fundamental unity of experience which the other philosophers had not recognized. He called this the **Word** or **logos** which he believed operated in the world through the constant changing of opposites into one another. He considered fire the most important element, symbolizing this eternal change. Heraclitus became disillusioned with his fellow citizens when they chose to remove a prominent figure from office. He did not think that most people knew what they were doing, and were quick to accept tradition or go along with the opinions of others. For this reason, he was in favour of an **aristocratic government (aristos)** rather than a **democracy** exclaiming "One person is ten thousand to me if he is best." His disillusionment with others, who could not understand his philosophy, led him ultimately to live a life of solitude in the mountains and to be known also as "**The Weeping Philosopher**."

Model Questions

- Explain the Philosophy of Heraclitus.
- Briefly narrate the life sketch of Heraclitus.
- Distinguish the ideas of Heraclitus with anyone of contemporary philosophers.
- Narrate the Cosmological elements of Pythagoras's philosophy?
- Critically analyse the Heraclitus 's thoughts on War and Aristocracy.
- How Heraclitus perceiving human knowledge and wisdom?

References

1. Barnes, Jonathan. The Presocratic Philosophers. London: Routledge & Kegan Paul, 1982
2. Graham, Daniel W. "Heraclitus' Criticism of Ionian Philosophy." Oxford Studies in Ancient Philosophy 15 (1997): 1-50.
3. http://www.philosimply.com/philosopher/heraclitus
4. http://www.spaceandmotion.com/philosophy-metaphysics-heraclitus.htm
5. https://classicalwisdom.com/heraclitus-fire-flux/
6. https://en.wikipedia.org/wiki/Heraclitus
7. https://philosophyforchange.wordpress.com/2008/04/07/heraclitus-on-change/
8. https://plato.stanford.edu/entries/heraclitus/
9. https://www.ancient.eu/article/183/heraclitus-life-is-flux/
10. https://www.britannica.com/biography/Heraclitus
11. https://www.iep.utm.edu/heraclit/
12. https://www.philosophybasics.com/philosophers_heraclitus.html

13. Hussey, Edward. "Epistemology and Meaning in Heraclitus." Language and Logos. Ed. M. Schofield and M. C. Nussbaum. Cambridge: Cambridge UP, 1982. 33-59.
14. Kahn, Charles H. The Art and Thought of Heraclitus. Cambridge: Cambridge UP, 1979.
15. Kirk, G. S. Heraclitus: The Cosmic Fragments. Cambridge: Cambridge UP, 1954.
16. Marcovich, Miroslav. Heraclitus: Greek Text with a Short Commentary. Merida, Venezuela: U. of the Andes, 1967.
17. Mourelatos, Alexander P. D. "Heraclitus, Parmenides, and the Naive Metaphysics of Things." Exegesis and Argument. Ed. E. N. Lee et al. Assen: Van Gorcum, 1973. 16-48.
18. Nussbaum, Martha C. "Psychê in Heraclitus." Phronesis 17 (1972): 1-16, 153-70.
19. Robinson, T. M. Heraclitus: Fragments. Toronto: U of Toronto P, 1987.
20. Vlastos, Gregory. "On Heraclitus." American Journal of Philology 76 (1955): 337-68. Reprinted in G. Vlastos, Studies in Greek Philosophy, vol. 1, Princeton: Princeton U. Pr., 1995.

Chapter - 11

Parmenides

Introduction

Parmenides of Elea was a **Presocratic** Greek philosopher. As the first philosopher to inquire into the nature of existence itself, he is incontrovertibly credited as the "**Father of Metaphysics**." As the first to employ deductive, a priori arguments to justify his claims, he competes with **Aristotle** for the title "Father of Logic." He is the founder of the "**Eleatic School**" of thought - a philosophical label ascribed to Presocratics who purportedly argued that reality is in some sense a unified and unchanging singular entity. This has often been understood to mean there is just one thing in all of existence. In light of this questionable interpretation, Parmenides has traditionally been viewed as a pivotal figure in the history of philosophy: one who challenged the physical systems of his predecessors and set forth for his successors the metaphysical criteria any successful system must meet. Other thinkers, also commonly thought of as **Eleatics**, include: **Zeno** of Elea, **Melissus** of Samos, and **Xenophanes** of Colophon.

Parmenides' only written work is a **poem** entitled, supposedly, but likely erroneously, On Nature. Only a limited number of "fragments" of his poem are still in existence, which have traditionally been assigned to three main sections - **Proem**, **Reality**, and **Opinion**. The Proem (prelude) features a young man on a **cosmic journey** in search of enlightenment, expressed in traditional Greek religious motifs and geography. This is followed by the central, most philosophically-oriented section. Here, Parmenides positively endorses certain epistemic guidelines for inquiry, which he then uses to argue for his famous metaphysical claims - that "what is" cannot be in motion, change, come-to-be, perish, lack uniformity, and so forth. The final section (Opinion) concludes the poem with a **theogonical** and **cosmogonical** account of the world, which paradoxically employs the very phenomena that Reality seems to have denied. Furthermore, despite making apparently true claims (for example, the moon gets its light from the sun), the account offered in Opinion is supposed to be representative of the mistaken "opinions of mortals," and thus is to be rejected on some level.

All three sections of the poem seem particularly contrived to yield a cohesive and unified thesis. However, discerning exactly what that thesis is supposed to be has proven a vexing, perennial problem since ancient times. Even Plato expressed reservations as to whether Parmenides' "noble depth" could be understood at all - and Plato possessed Parmenides' entire poem, a blessing denied to modern scholars. Although there are many important philological and philosophical questions surrounding Parmenides' poem, the central question for Parmenidean studies is addressing how the positively-endorsed, radical conclusions of Reality can be adequately reconciled with the seemingly contradictory cosmological account Parmenides rejects in Opinion.

As with other ancient figures, little can be said about Parmenides' life with much confidence. It is certain that his hometown was **Elea** - a Greek settlement along the Tyrrhenian coast of the Appenine Peninsula, just south of the Bay of Salerno, now located in the modern municipality of Ascea, Italy. Herodotus reports that members of the Phocaean tribe established this settlement 540-535 B.C., and thus Parmenides was of Ionian stock. Parmenides' father, a wealthy aristocrat named **Pyres**, was probably one of the original colonizers.

Parmenides was remained a lifelong citizen and permanent resident of Elea. Several sources attest that he established a set of laws for Elea, which remained in effect and sworn to for centuries after his death. A pedestal discovered in Elea is dedicated to him, with an inscription crediting him not only as a "natural philosopher," but as a member of a local healing cult. Thus, he likely contributed to the healing arts as a patron and practitioner. Finally, if Parmenides really was a personal teacher of **Zeno of Elea** (490-430 B.C.E)., Parmenides must have been present in Elea well into the mid-fourth century B.C.E. However, when and where Parmenides died is entirely unattested.

Work

Parmenides' only known work, a **poem** written in **hexameter** verse around 475 B.C. and entitled "**On Nature**", has only survived in fragmentary form, with approximately 150 of the original 3,000 lines of text remaining today. It is divided into two main sections, describing the two ways or two views of reality, "**The Way of Truth**" and "**The Way of Appearance/Opinion**", along with an introduction. Parmenides argued in favour of the Way of Truth and against The Way of Appearance. In the poem, Parmenides argued that the every-day perception of the reality of the physical world is mistaken, and that the reality of the world is "the One", an unchanging, ungenerated, indestructible whole. Likewise, the phenomena of movement and change are simply appearances of the real static, eternal reality. He further asserted that the truth cannot be known through sensory perception, only through **pure reason**.

Parmenides set out the heart of his case in a **worldview** that is, according to Aristotle, "near to madness". He argued as follows: "What-is-not" does not exist. Since anything that comes into being must arise out of "what-is-not", objects cannot come into being. Likewise, they cannot pass away, because in order to do so they would have to enter the realm of "what-is-not". Since it does not exist, "what-is-not" cannot be the womb of generation, or the tomb of that which perishes. The "no-longer" and the "not-yet" are therefore variants of "what-is-not", and so the past and future do not exist either. Change, then, is impossible. Equally, his argument continued, multiplicity is unreal, because the empty space necessary to separate one object from another would be another example of "what-is-not". And since things cannot be anything to a greater or lesser degree, the universe must be homogeneous, a single, undifferentiated, unchanging unity. Also, it must be finite and spherical, for it cannot be in one direction any more than in another.

Thus, by a strictly deductive argument, Parmenides asserted that change is impossible, and that coming-into-existence or ceasing-to-exist are likewise impossible, so that everything that exists is permanent, ungenerated, indestructible and unchanging. His argument refutes all accounts of the origin of the world, and represents an early type of **Monism**. Parmenides therefore made the ontological argument against nothingness, essentially denying the possible existence of a void, which led **Leucippus** and **Democritus** to propose their theory of **Atomism** specifically to contradict his argument.

The Philosophy

The distinction between the **Way of Truth** and the **Way of Seeming** is the first attempt in Greek philosophy to distinguish between reality and appearance, or essence and phenomena, which had lasting effects on the subsequent history of Western philosophy.

In the Way of Truth, Parmenides presented his **ontology**: a real being is timeless, immobile, immutable, permanent, unborn, imperishable, one, and whole. Parmenides did not discuss what that was, which exists permanently, but highlighted the fact of existence as the truth.

There is only one other description of the way remaining, namely, that **What Is**. To this way there are very many sign-posts: that Being has no coming-into-being and no destruction, for it is whole of limb, without motion, and without end. And it never Was, nor Will be, because it Is now, a Whole all together, One, continuous; for what creation of it will you look for? One should both say and think that Being Is; for To Be is possible, and Nothingness is not possible.

Parmenides represented the real being as a **sphere**, a symbol of perfection for the Greeks. But since there is a (spatial) Limit, it is complete on every side, like the mass of a well rounded sphere, equally balanced from its centre in every direction; for it is not bound to be at all either greater or less in this direction or that.

In the Way of Seeming, Parmenides dismissed changes and motion as illusory, which we experience as real in everyday life. In everyday parlance, we speak of absence, void, and non-being or non-existence as if they are real. Coming into being is perceived as a process from non-being to being, and disappearance from being to non-being. For Parmenides, non-being in a genuine sense is a total absence or a sheer nothing that cannot be in principle an object of thought. What we can think of has existence by the fact of being thought. The moment one thinks something, an object of thought is posited as a being. Thinking inherently involves positing an object of thought.

To think is the same as the thought that It Is; for you will not find thinking without Being, in (regard to) which there is an expression. Parmenides presented a view of truth, which is known as a correspondence theory of truth. In this view, truth is defined as the accordance of idea with reality. Since Parmenides conceived the eternal and unchanging being as the sole reality, true knowledge is a realization of this being and this knowledge is attainable not by senses but by reason alone.

For this (view) can never predominate, that **That Which I** Not exists. You must debar your thought from this way of search, nor let ordinary experience in its variety force you along this way, the eyes, sightless as it is, and the ear, full of sound, and the tongue, to rule; but judge by means of the Reason the much-contested proof which is expounded by me.

In our everyday discourse, we distinguish beings according to their kind, mode, and sense of existence. Diversity of beings is established based upon differences in these existential characteristics. What is common to all beings is the fact of existence. Parmenides conceived the fact of existence as the common denominator to all beings and conceptualized it as the One. True knowledge is the realization of the fact of to-be as the first principle of being. Our perception of diversity among beings is, for Parmenides, merely a view of mortals in the World of Seeming.

Overview of Parmenides' Poem

Ancient tradition holds that Parmenides produced only one written work, which was supposedly entitled **On Nature**. This title is suspect, as it had become common even by Sextus' time to attribute this generic title to all Presocratic works. No copy of the original work has survived, in any part. Instead, scholars have collected purported quotations from a number of ancient authors and attempted to reconstruct the poem by arranging these fragments according to internal and external evidence. The result is a rather fragmentary text, constituted by approximately 154 dactylic-hexameter lines. This reconstructed arrangement has then been traditionally divided into three distinct parts: an introductory section known as the **Proem**; a central section of epistemological guidelines and **metaphysical arguments**; and a concluding "cosmology".

The linear order of the three main extant sections is certain, and the assignment of particular fragments to each section is generally well-supported. However, it must be admitted that confidence in the connectedness, completeness, and internal ordering of the fragments in each section decreases significantly as one proceeds through the poem linearly: *Proem-Reality-Opinion*. Furthermore, many philological difficulties persist throughout the reconstruction. There are conflicting transmissions regarding which Greek word to read, variant punctuation possibilities, concerns surrounding adequate translation, ambiguities in the poetical form, and so forth. Given all of this, any serious engagement with Parmenides' work should begin by acknowledging the incomplete status of the text and recognizing that interpretative certainty is generally not to be found.

Parmenides' poem began with a proem describing a journey he figuratively once made to the abode of a goddess. He described how he was conveyed on "the far-fabled path of the divinity" in a chariot by a team of mares and how the maiden daughters of Helios, the sun-god, led the way. These maidens take Parmenides to whence they themselves have come, to "the halls of Night", before which stand "the gates of the paths of night and day". The maidens gently persuade Justice, guardian of these gates, to open them so that Parmenides himself may pass through to the abode within.

Parmenides thus describes how the goddess who dwells there welcomed him upon his arrival.

Parmenides' proem is no epistemological allegory of enlightenment but a topographically specific description of a mystical journey to the halls of Night. In **Hesiod**, the "horrible dwelling of dark Night" is where the goddesses Night and Day alternately reside as the other traverses the sky above the Earth. Both Parmenides' and Hesiod's conception of this place have their precedent in the Babylonian mythology of the sun god's abode. This abode also traditionally served as a place of judgment, and this fact tends to confirm that when Parmenides' goddess tells him that no ill fate has sent him ahead to this place, she is indicating that he has miraculously reached the place to which travel the souls of the dead.

In the proem, then, Parmenides casts himself in the role of an initiate into the kind of mysteries that were during his day part of the religious milieu of **Magna Graecia**. The motif of the initiate is important, for it informs Parmenides' portrayal of himself as one whose encounter with a major divinity has yielded a special knowledge or wisdom. The divinity in this instance would seem to be Night herself: Parmenides goes to "the halls of Night", and the goddess who greets him welcomes him to "our home". The goddess Night serves as counsellor to Zeus in some of the major Orphic cosmologies, including the Derveni cosmology. In the closely related Orphic Rhapsodies, Night instructs Zeus on how to preserve the unity produced by his absorption of all things into himself as he sets about initiating a new **cosmogonic phase**. It is thus appropriate that Night should be the source of Parmenides' revelation, for Parmenidean metaphysics is very much concerned with the principle of unity in the cosmos.

Thoughts on Reality

Immediately following the **Proem**, the poem moves into its central philosophical section: **Reality**. In this section, Parmenides' positively endorsed epistemic and metaphysical claims are outlined. Though lengthy quotations strongly suggest a certain internal structure, there is certainly some room for debate with respect to proper placement, in particular amongst the shorter fragments that do not share any common content with the others. In any case, due to the overall relative completeness of the section and its clearly novel philosophical content these lines have received far more attention from philosophically-minded readers, in both ancient and modern times.

In Reality, the unnamed youth is first informed that there are only two logically possible "routes of inquiry" one might embark upon in order to understand "reality". Parmenides' goddess endorses the first route, which recognizes that "what-is" is, and that it must be (it is not to not be), on the grounds that it is completely trustworthy and persuasive. On the other hand, the goddess warns the youth away from the route which posits "what-is-not and necessarily cannot be," as it is a path that can neither be known nor spoken of. The reasoning seems to be that along this latter route, there is no concept to conceive of, no subject there to refer to, and no properties that can be predicated of - "nothingness."

In the third possible "route of inquiry", the goddess seems to warn the youth from following the path which holds being and not-being to be both the same and not the same. This is the path that mortals are said to wander "without judgment," on a "backwards-turning journey." Not only is confusing "what is" and "what is not" different from positing necessary being and non-being, and thus a distinct "route," but this description also seems to correspond far better to the cosmogony of opposites found in Opinion than to the route of "what is not and necessarily cannot be."

The order not to follow the path that posits only "what is" is further complicated by the fragmentary report that there is some sort of close relationship between thinking and being: "...for thinking and being are the same thing," or "...for the same thing is for thinking as is for being". Scholars are divided as to what the exact meaning of this relationship is supposed to be, leading to numerous mutually exclusive interpretative models. Does Parmenides really mean to make an identity claim between the two - that thinking really is numerically one and the same as being, and vice-versa? Or, is it that there is some shared properties between the two? Is Parmenides making the rather problematic claim that whatever can be thought, exists? Or, more charitably, only that whatever does exist can in principle be thought of without contradiction, and thus is understandable by reason - unlike "nothingness"? Perhaps both? Most commonly, Parmenides has been understood here as anticipating Russellian concerns with language and how meaning and reference must be coextensive with, and even preceded by, **ontology**.

In any case, from these epistemic considerations, the goddess' deductive arguments are supposed to follow with certainty from deductive, a priori reasoning. By studiously avoiding thinking in any way which entails thinking about "what-is-not," via reductio, the subject of Reality is concluded to be: truly eternal- ungenerated and imperishable, a continuous whole, unmoved and unique, perfect and uniform. For instance, since coming-to-be involves positing "not-being" in the past, and mutatis mutandis for perishing, and since "not-being" cannot be conceived of, "what is" cannot have either property. In a similar vein, spatial motion includes "not-being" at a current location in the past, and thus motion is also denied. This line of reasoning can be readily advanced to deny any sort of change at all.

In the end, what is certain about Reality is that there is purportedly at least one thing that must possess all the aforementioned "perfect" properties, and that these properties are supposed to follow from some problem with thinking about "what is not." It has been commonly inferred from this that Parmenides advocated that there is actually just one thing in the entire world, and that this entity necessarily possesses the aforementioned properties.

Summary

Parmenides of Elea was an early Pre-Socratic Greek philosopher and founder and chief representative of the **Eleatic School** of ancient Greek philosophy. He is one of the most significant, influential, most difficult and obscure among the Pre-Socratic philosophers, and he is sometimes referred to as the **father of Metaphysics**. He particularly influenced **Plato**, who always spoke of him with veneration. Perhaps his greatest contribution to philosophy was his method of reasoned proof for assertions. In denying the reality of change as part of his **Monist philosophy**, Parmenides presented a turning point in the history of Western Philosophy, and sparked a philosophical challenge that determined the course of enquiries of subsequent philosophers such as **Empedocles**, **Anaxagoras** and **Democritus**, and an intellectual revolution that still echoes today.

Model Questions

1. Explain the Philosophy of Parmenides.
2. Briefly narrate the life sketch of Parmenides.
3. Distinguish the ideas of Parmenides with anyone of contemporary philosophers.
4. Narrate the metaphysical elements of Parmenides' philosophy?
5. Critically analyse the Parmenides' thoughts on reality.
6. Why Parmenides credited as father of metaphysics?

References

1. Cassin, B., 1998. Parménide: Sur la nature ou sur l'Étant. La langue de l'étre, Paris: Éditions de Seuil.
2. Conche, M., 1996. Parménide. Le Poème: Fragments, Paris: Presses Universitaires de France.
3. Cordero, N.-L., 1984. Les Deux Chemins de Parménide: Édition critique, traduction, études et bibliografie, Paris: J. Vrin; Brussels: Éditions Ousia.
4. Coxon, A. H., 2009. The Fragments of Parmenides: A critical text with introduction, translation, the ancient testimonia and a commentary, revised and expanded edition with new translations by Richard McKirahan, Las Vegas/Zurich/Athens: Parmenides Publishing.
5. Diels, H., and W. Kranz, Die Fragmente der Vorsokratiker, 6th edn. Berlin: Weidmann, 1951–52.
6. Gallop, D., 1984. Parmenides of Elea: Fragments, Toronto: University of Toronto Press.
7. http://www.iep.utm.edu/parmenid/
8. http://www.newworldencyclopedia.org/entry/Parmenides
9. http://www.philosimply.com/philosopher/parmenides
10. https://en.wikipedia.org/wiki/Parmenides
11. https://plato.stanford.edu/entries/parmenides/
12. https://www.ancient.eu/Parmenides/

13. https://www.britannica.com/biography/Parmenides-Greek-philosopher
14. https://www.ontology.co/parmenides.htm
15. https://www.philosophybasics.com/philosophers_parmenides.html
16. https://www.youtube.com/watch?reload=9&v=MbDW1836TXg
17. Kirk, G. S., J. E. Raven, and M. Schofield, 1983. The Presocratic Philosophers, 2nd edn., Cambridge: Cambridge University Press, Chapter VIII: "Parmenides of Elea."
18. O'Brien, D. (with J. Frère), 1987. Le Poème de Parménide: Texte, Traduction, Essai Critique = P. Aubenque (gen. ed.), Études sur Parménide, i. Paris: J. Vrin.
19. Reale, G., and Ruggiu, L., 1991. Parmenide. Poema sulla natura. I frammenti e le testimonianze indirette, Milan: Rusconi.
20. Tarán, L., 1965. Parmenides: A Text with Translation, Commentary, and Critical Essays, Princeton: Princeton University Press.

Chapter - 12

Stoicism

Introduction

Stoicism is an ancient Greek philosophy developed by **Zeno of Citium** around 300 B.C. as a refinement of **Cynicism** which teaches the development of self-control and fortitude as a means of overcoming destructive emotions. It does not seek to extinguish emotions competely, but rather seeks to transform them by a resolute **Asceticism**, which enables a person to develop clear judgment, inner calm and freedom from suffering. Stoicism is not just a set of beliefs or ethical claims, but rather a way of life, involving constant practice and training, and incorporating the practice of logic, **Socratic dialogue** and self-dialogue, contemplation of death, and a kind of meditation aimed at training one's attention to remain in the present moment.

The term "**stoic**" was taken from the "**stoa poikile**" (meaning "painted porch") where Zeno of Citium used to teach. In modern usage, the word refers to someone who is unemotional or indifferent to pain, pleasure, grief or joy, and has little in common with its philosophical roots. As an ethical doctrine, the goal of Stoicism is freedom from passion through the pursuit of reason and "apatheia". It teaches indifference and a "passive" reaction to external events and equanimity in the face of life's highs and lows.

The Stoics taught that becoming a clear, unbiased and self-disciplined thinker allows one to understand the "**logos**" (the natural universal reason in all things). Thus, unhappiness and evil are the results of ignorance, and if someone is unkind, it is because they are unaware of their own universal reason. The solution to this evil and unhappiness can be achieved through the practice of Stoic philosophy. Hence the famous Stoic maxim: "Live according to nature", both in the sense of the laws of the universe and of man's own essential nature, reason. In many respects, it bears a remarkable similarity to the ethical teaching of **Siddhartha Gautama** (c. 563 - 483 B.C.) and **Buddhism**, which is grounded in the four noble truths: (1) all life has suffering; (2) suffering is rooted in passion and desire; (3) happiness is freedom from the passions; (4) moral restraint and self-discipline is the means by which one becomes free from suffering.

An important aspect of Stoicism involves improving the individual's ethical and moral well-being by having a will which is in agreement with Nature, and by practising the four cardinal virtues (derived from the teachings of **Plato**: **wisdom** ("sophia"), **courage** ("andreia"), **justice** ("dikaiosyne") and **temperance** ("sophrosyne"). For the Stoics, living according to reason and virtue is to live in harmony with the divine order of the universe, and recognizing the common reason and essential value of all people. They therefore promoted **Egalitarianism**, and, unusually for their day, encouraged the acceptance of even slaves as equals on the grounds that all are the "sons of God", echoing Socrates' claim that "I am not an Athenian or a Greek, but a citizen of the world". They also denied the importance of external differences such as rank and wealth in social relationships.

To some extent, Stoicism assumes **Determinism** in that it holds that we will in any case do as the necessity of the world compels us, but it holds that we should not merely obey the law, but assent to our own obedience and follow the law consciously and deliberately, as only a rational being can.

The 1st Century AD Roman philosopher and Stoic, **Seneca the Younger** (4 B.C. - A.D. 65), the most famous and popular philosopher of his day, took the subject of anger seriously enough to dedicate a whole book to the subject. He saw anger as a philosophical problem and amenable to treatment by philosophical argument, not just an irrational outburst over which we have no control. He thought that anger arose from holding overly optimistic ideas about the world, leading to unrealistic expectations, and advised a more pessimistic attitude so that one was mentally prepared for the kinds of bad things that happen, which would therefore not lead to such outbursts of anger.

Philosophical Antecedents

Stoicism is a **Hellenistic** eudaimonic philosophy, which means that we can expect it to be influenced by its immediate predecessors and contemporaries, as well as to be in open critical dialogue with them. These includes Socratic thinking, as it has arrived to us mainly through the early Platonic dialogues; the Platonism of the Academic school, particularly in its Skeptical phase; Aristotelianism of the Peripatetic school; Cynicism; Skepticism; and Epicureanism. It is worth noting, in order to put things into context, that a quantitative study of extant records concerning known philosophers of the ancient Greco-Roman world estimates that the leading schools of the time were, in descending order: **Academics-Platonists** (19%), **Stoics** (12%), **Epicureans** (8%), and **Peripatetics-Aristotelians** (6%).

Eudaimonia was the term that meant a life worth living, often translated nowadays as "happiness" in the broad sense, or more appropriately, flourishing. For the Greco-Romans this often involved excellence at moral virtues. The idea is therefore closely related to that of virtue ethics, an approach most famously associated with **Aristotle** and his **Nicomachean Ethics**, and revived in modern times by a number of philosophers, including Philippa Foot (2001) and **Alasdair MacIntyre** (2013).

Stoicism is best understood in the context of the differences among some of the similar schools of the time. **Socrates** had argued that virtue, and in particular the four cardinal virtues of wisdom, courage, justice and temperance, are the only good. Everything else is neither good nor bad in and of itself. By contrast, for Aristotle the virtues were necessary but not sufficient for eudaimonia. One also needed a certain degree of positive goods, such as health, wealth, education, and even a bit of good looks. In other words, **Aristotle** expounded the rather commonsensical notion that a flourishing life is part effort, because one can and ought to cultivate one's character, and part luck, in the form of the physical and cultural conditions that affect and shape one's life.

Contrast this to the rather extreme take of the **Cynics**, who not only thought that virtue was the only good, like **Socrates**, but that the additional goods that Aristotle was worried about were actually distractions and needed to be positively avoided. Cynics like Diogenes of Sinope were famous for their ascetic and shall we say rather eclectic life style, as is epitomized by a story about him told by **Diogenes Laertius**: "One day, observing a child drinking out of his hands, he cast away the cup from his wallet with the words, 'A child has beaten me in plainness of living.'"

One way to think of this is that the Aristotelian approach comes across as a bit too aristocratic: if one does not have certain privileges in life, one cannot achieve **eudaimonia**. By contrast, the Cynics were preaching a rather extremely minimalist life style, which is hard to practice for most human beings. What the Stoics tried to do, then, was to strike a balance in the middle, by endorsing the twin crucial ideas, on which I will elaborate later, that virtue is the only true good, in itself sufficient for eudaimonia regardless of one's circumstances, but also that other things may be rationally preferred (**Proegmena**) or "dispreferred" (**Apoproegmena**), as in the case of sickness, ignorance, and poverty, as long as one did not confuse them for things with inherent value.

Greek Stoicism

The "Greek" phase of the Stoa covers the first and second periods, from the founding of the school by Zeno to the shifting of the centre of gravity from Athens to Rome in the time of Posidonius in the I Century B.C.E., who became a friend of Cicero. Stoicism was not just born, but flourished in **Athens**, even though most of its exponents originated from the Eastern Mediterranean: **Zeno** from Citium (modern Cyprus), **Cleanthes** from Assos (modern Western Turkey), and **Chrysippus** from Soli (modern Southern Turkey), among others.

From the beginning Stoicism was squarely a "Socratic" philosophy, and the Stoics themselves did not mind such a label. Zeno began his studies under the Cynic Crates, and Cynicism always had a strong influence on Stoicism, all the way to the later writings of Epictetus. But Zeno also counted among his teachers Polemo, the head of the Academy, and Stilpo, of the Megarian school founded by Euclid of Megaria, a pupil of Socrates. This is relevant because Zeno came to elaborate a philosophy that was both of clear Socratic inspiration and a compromise between Polemo's and Stilpo's positions, as the first one endorsed the idea that there are external goods while the second one claimed that nothing external can be good or bad. That compromise consisted in the uniquely Stoic notion that external goods are of ethically neutral value, but are nonetheless the object of natural pursuit.

Zeno established the tripartite study of Stoic philosophy comprising ethics, physics and logic. The ethics was basically a moderate version of Cynicism; the physics was influenced by Plato's **Timaeus** and encompassed a universe permeated by an active and a passive principle, as well as a cosmic web of cause and effect; the logic included both what we today refer to as formal logic and epistemology, that is, a theory of knowledge, which for the Stoics was decidedly empiricist-naturalistic.

The Stoics after Zeno disagreed on a number of issues, often interpreting Zeno's teachings differently. Perhaps the most important example is provided by the dispute between Cleanthes and Chrysippus about the unity of the virtues: Zeno had talked about each virtue in turn being a kind of wisdom, which Cleanthes interpreted in a strict unitary sense, while **Chrysippus** understood in a more pluralistic fashion. The early Stoics could also be stubbornly anti-empirical in their apologetics of Zeno's writings, as when Chrysippus insisted in defending the idea that the heart, not the brain, is the seat of intelligence. This went against pretty conclusive anatomical evidence that was already available in the Hellenistic period, and earned the Stoics the scorn of Galen, though later Stoics did update their beliefs on the matter.

Despite this faux pas, **Chrysippus** was arguably the most influential Stoic thinker, responsible for an overhaul of the school, which had declined under the guidance of **Cleanthes**, a broad systematization of its teachings, and the introduction of a number of novel notions in logic the aspect of Stoicism that has had the most technical philosophical impact in the long run.

In the six decades following Chrysippus there were just two heads of the Stoa, Zeno of Tarsus (south-central Turkey) and Diogenes of Babylon, whose contributions were rather less significant than those of Chrysippus himself. We have to wait until 155 B.C.E. for the next impactful event, when the heads of the three major schools in **Athens** were sent by the city to Rome in order to help with diplomatic efforts. The philosophers in question, including the Stoic Diogenes of Babylon, made a huge impression on the Roman public with their public performances, paving the road for the later shift of philosophy from Athens to Rome, as well as other centres of learning, like **Alexandria**.

Beginning with Antipater of Tarsus, and then more obviously **Panaetius** and **Posidonius**, the Stoics revisited their relationship with the Academy, especially in light of the above mentioned importance of the Timaeus for Stoic cosmology. Apparently, what particularly interested Posidonius was the fact that Plato's main character in the dialogue is a Pythagorean, a school that Posidonius somewhat anachronistically managed to link to Stoicism.

It appears that the broader project pursued by both Panaetius and Posidonius was one of seeking common ground among Academicism, Aristotelianism and Stoicism itself, that is, the three branches of Socratic philosophy. This process seems to have been in part responsible for the further success of Stoicism once the major philosophers of the various schools moved from Athens to Rome, after the **Diaspora** of 88-86 B.C.E.

Roman Stoicism

If the visit to Rome by the head of various philosophical schools in 155 B.C.E. was crucial for bringing philosophy to the attention of the Romans, the political events of 88-86 B.C.E. changed the course of Western philosophy in general, and Stoicism in particular, for the remainder of antiquity. At that time philosophers, particularly the Peripatetic Athenion and the Epicurean Aristion, were politically in charge at Athens, and made the crucial mistake of siding with Mithridates against Rome. The defeat of the King of Pontus, and consequently of Athens, spelled disaster for the latter and led to a Diaspora of philosophers throughout the **Mediterranean**.

To be fair, we have no evidence of the continuation of the **Stoa** as an actual school in Athens after **Panaetius**, and we know that **Posidonius** taught in Rhodes, not Athens. However, according to Sedley (2003), it was the events of 88-86 B.C.E. that finally and permanently moved the center of gravity of Stoicism away from its Greek cradle to Rome, **Rhodes**, and Tarsus, where a Stoic was at one point chosen by Augustus to govern the city.

Most crucially, however, Stoicism became important in Rome during the fraught time of the transition between the late Republic and the Empire, with Cato the Younger eventually becoming a role model for later Stoics because of his political opposition to the "tyrant" Julius Caesar. Sedley highlights two Stoic philosophers of the late First Century B.C.E., Athenodorus of Tarsus and Arius Didymus, as precursors of one of the greatest and most controversial Stoic figures, Seneca. Both Athenodorus and Arius were personal counsellors to the first emperor, Augustus, and Arius even wrote a letter of consolation to Livia, Augustus' wife, addressing the death of her son, which Seneca later hailed as a reference work of emotional therapy, the sort of work he himself engaged in and became famous for.

Once we get to the Imperial period, we see a decided shift away from the more theoretical aspects of Stoicism and toward more practical treatments of the ethics. However, as Gill points out, this should not lead us to think that the vitality of Stoicism had taken a nose dive by then: we know of a number of new treatises produced by Stoic writers of that period, on everything ranging from ethics to physics, and the Summary of the Traditions of Greek Theology by **Cornutus** is one of a handful of complete Stoic treatises to survive from any period of the history of the school. Still, it is certainly the case that the best known Stoics of the time were either teachers like Musonius Rufus and **Epictetus**, or politically active, like **Seneca** and **Marcus** Aurelius, thus shaping our understanding of the period as a contrast to the foundational and more theoretical one of Zeno and Chrysippus.

Importantly, it is from the late Republic and Empire that we also get some of the best indirect sources on Stoicism, particularly several books by Cicero and Diogenes Laertius' Lives of the Eminent Philosophers. And this literature went on to influence later writers well after the decline of Stoicism, particularly Plotinus (205-270 C.E.) and even the 6th Century C.E. Neoplatonist Simplicius.

All of the above notwithstanding, what is most vital about Stoicism during the Roman Imperial period, however, is also what arguably made the philosophy's impact reverberate throughout the centuries, eventually leading to two revivals, the so-called **Neostoicism** of the Renaissance, and the current "modern Stoicism" movement. The sources of such vitality were fundamentally two: on the one hand charismatic teachers like **Musonius** and **Epictetus**, and on the other hand influential political figures like Seneca and Marcus. Indeed, Musonius was, in a sense, both: not only he was a member of the Roman "knight" class, and the teacher of Epictetus, he was also politically active, openly criticizing the policies of both Nero and Vespasian, and getting exiled twice as a result. Others were not so lucky: Stoic philosophers suffered a series of persecutions from displeased emperors, which resulted in murders or exile for a number of them, especially during the reigns of Nero, Vespasian and Domitian. Seneca famously had to commit suicide on Nero's orders, and Epictetus was exiled to Greece by **Domitian**.

It is also important to appreciate different "styles" of being Stoic among the major Roman figures. As Gill (2003) points out, Epictetus was rather strict, arching back to the Cynic model of quasi-asceticism. Musonius was a sometimes odd combination of "conservative" and "progressive" Stoic, advocating the importance of marriage and family, but also stating very clearly that women are just as capable of practicing virtue. **Seneca** was not only more open to the pursuit of "preferred indifferents", but explicitly stated that he was critical of some of the doctrines of the early Stoics, and that he was open to learn from other schools, including the Epicureans. Famously, Marcus Aurelius was open about theology, at several points in the *Meditabtions* (1997) explicitly stating the two alternatives of "Providence" (Stoic doctrine) or "Atoms" (the Epicurean take), for instance: "Either there is a fatal necessity and invincible order, or a kind Providence, or a confusion without a purpose and without a director. If then there is an invincible necessity, why do you resist? But if there is a Providence that allows itself to be propitiated, make yourself worthy of the help of the divinity. But if there is a confusion without a governor, be content that in such a tempest you have yourself a certain ruling intelligence"; or: "With respect to what may happen to you from without, consider that it happens either by chance or according to Providence, and you must neither blame chance nor accuse Providence". More is said about this specific topic in the section on Stoic metaphysics and teleology.

There is ample evidence, then, that Stoicism was alive and well during the Roman period, although the emphasis did shift from laying down the fundamental ideas to refining them and putting them into practice, both in personal and social life.

Summary

Stoicism originated as a Hellenistic philosophy, founded in Athens by Zeno of Citium. It was influenced by Socrates and the Cynics, and it engaged in vigorous debates with the Skeptics, the Academics, and the Epicureans. The name comes from the Stoa Poikile, or painted porch, an open market in Athens where the original Stoics used to meet and teach philosophy. Stoicism moved to Rome where it flourished during the period of the Empire, alternatively being persecuted by Emperors who disliked it and openly embraced by Emperors who attempted to live by it. It influenced **Christianity**, as well as a number of major philosophical figures throughout the ages, and in the early 21st century saw a revival as a practical philosophy associated with **Cognitive Behavioral Therapy** and similar approaches. Stoicism is a type of eudaimonic virtue ethics, asserting that the practice of virtue is both necessary and sufficient to achieve happiness. However, the Stoics also recognized the existence of "indifferents" (to eudaimonia) that could nevertheless be preferred or dispreferred, because they had planning value with respect to the ability to practice virtue. Stoicism was very much a philosophy meant to be applied to everyday living, focused on **ethics**, which was in turn informed by what the Stoics called "physics" and what they called "logic".

Model Questions

1. Explain the Philosophy of Stoicism.
2. Briefly narrate the origin of Stoicism.
3. Distinguish the ideas of Stoicism and Buddhism.
4. Narrate the reality elements of Stoicism?
5. Critically analyse implications of Stoicism in our day to day life.
6. How Roman and Greek Stoicism differ?

References

1. Arnim, H., 1903–5 Stoicorum Veterum Fragmenta Leipzig: Teubner (Volume 4 indexes, 1924).
2. Bowen, A. and Todd, R., 2004, Cleomedes' Lectures on Astronomy, Berkeley: University of California Press.
3. Dufour, Richard, 2004, Chrysippe. Oeuvre philosophique, 2 volumes, Paris: Les Belles Lettres
4. Edelstein, L. and Kidd, I.G., 1972, Posidonius, 2 vols. Cambridge: Cambridge University Press.
5. https://dailystoic.com/what-is-stoicism-a-definition-3-stoic-exercises-to-get-you-started/
6. https://en.wikipedia.org/wiki/Stoicism
7. https://plato.stanford.edu/entries/stoicism/?PHPSESSID=1127ae96bb5f45f15b3ec6577c2f6b9f
8. https://www.britannica.com/topic/Stoicism
9. https://www.iep.utm.edu/stoicism/
10. https://www.philosophybasics.com/branch_stoicism.html
11. https://www.youtube.com/watch?v=R9OCA6UFE-0
12. https://www.youtube.com/watch?v=yu7n0XzqtfA
13. Inwood, B. and Gerson, L., 1997, Hellenistic Philosophy 2nd ed. Indianapolis: Hackett Publishing 1997.

14. Inwood, B., 2007, Seneca: Selected Philosophical Letters translated with introduction and commentary. Oxford: Oxford University Press.
15. Long, A. A. and Sedley, D. N., 1987, The Hellenistic Philosophers 2 vols. Cambridge: Cambridge University Press
16. Nickel, R., 2009, Stoa und Stoiker. Auswahl der Fragmente und Zeugnisse, 2 volumes, Dusseldorf: Artemis und Winkler
17. Pomeroy, A., 1999, Arius Didymus: Epitome of Stoic Ethics, Atlanta: Society of Biblical Literature.
18. Ramelli, I. 2009, Hierocles the Stoic: Elements of Ethics, Fragments and Excerpts, Atlanta: Society of Biblical Literature.
19. Van Staaten, M., 1962, Panaetii Rhodii Fragmenta, Leiden: Brill.

Chapter - 13

Epicureanism

Introduction

Epicureanism is a system of philosophy based upon the teachings of the ancient Greek philosopher **Epicurus**, founded around 307 BC. Epicurus was an atomic materialist, following in the steps of **Democritus**. His materialism led him to a general attack on superstition and divine intervention. Following **Aristippus** Epicurus believed that what he called "**pleasure**" was the greatest good, but that the way to attain such pleasure was to live modestly, to gain knowledge of the workings of the world, and to limit one's desires. This would lead one to attain a state of tranquility (**ataraxia**) and freedom from fear as well as an absence of bodily pain (**aponia**). The combination of these two states constitutes happiness in its highest form. Although Epicureanism is a form of **hedonism** insofar as it declares pleasure to be its sole intrinsic goal, the concept that the absence of pain and fear constitutes the greatest pleasure, and its advocacy of a simple life, make it very different from "hedonism" as colloquially understood.

Epicureanism was originally a challenge to **Platonism**, though later it became the main opponent of Stoicism. Epicurus and his followers shunned politics. After the death of Epicurus, his school was headed by Hermarchus; later many Epicurean societies flourished in the Late Hellenistic era and during the Roman era. Its best-known Roman proponent was the poet **Lucretius**. By the end of the Roman

Empire, being opposed by philosophies that were now in the ascendant, Epicureanism had all but died out, and would be resurrected in the Age of **Enlightenment**.

Some writings by Epicurus have survived. Some scholars consider the epic poem ***On the Nature of Things*** by **Lucretius** to present in one unified work the core arguments and theories of Epicureanism. Many of the scrolls unearthed at the Villa of the Papyri at Herculaneum are Epicurean texts. At least some are thought to have belonged to the Epicurean Philodemus. Today, there are large Epicurean communities in **Greece**, a Society of Friends of Epicurus in the West, and the School has a growing online presence. In the French-speaking world, **Michel Onfray** is considered Neo-Epicurean.

The Nature of Epicureanism

Several fundamental concepts characterize the philosophy of Epicurus. In physics, these are atomism, a mechanical conception of causality, limited, however, by the idea of a spontaneous motion, or "swerve," of the atoms, which interrupts the necessary effect of a cause; the infinity of the universe and the equilibrium of all forces that circularly enclose its phenomena; and the existence of gods conceived as beatified and immortal natures completely extraneous to happenings in the world. In ethics, the basic concepts are the identification of good with pleasure and of the supreme good and ultimate end with the absence of pain from the body and the soul - a limit beyond which pleasure does not grow but changes; the reduction of every human relation to the principle of utility, which finds its highest expression in friendship, in which it is at the same time surmounted; and, in accordance with this end, the limitation of all desire and the practice of the virtues, from which pleasure is inseparable, and a withdrawn and quiet life.

In principle, Epicurus's **ethic of pleasure** is the exact opposite of the Stoic's **ethic of duty**. The consequences, however, are the same: in the end, the Epicurean is forced to live with the same temperance and justice as the Stoic. Of utmost importance, however, is one point of divergence: the walls of the Stoic's city are those of the world, and its law is that of reason; the limits of the Epicurean's city are those of a garden, and the law is that of friendship. Though this garden can also reach the boundaries of earth, its centre is always an individual.

Epicurus's predecessors were in physics **Leucippus** and **Democritus** and in ethics Antiphon Sophista, Aristippus of Cyrene, and Eudoxus of Cnidus, a geometer and astronomer. Epicurus differed from all of these in his systematic spirit and in the unity that he tried to give to every part of philosophy. In this respect, he was greatly influenced by the philosophy and teachings of **Aristotle** - taking over the essentials of his doctrines and pursuing the problems that he posed.

Happiness and Pleasure

While we have lost most of Epicurus' treatises on ethics and happiness, his basic ideas are very clearly outlined in his justly famous Letter to Menoeceus. He begins with a claim familiar from Plato and Aristotle: that we all desire happiness as an end in itself, and all other things are desired as a means for producing happiness. But what is happiness? Epicurus gives a straightforward definition, influenced by **Aristippus**, a disciple of **Socrates** and founder of the **Cyrenaic school** of philosophy: "Pleasure is our first and kindred good. It is the starting point of every choice and of every aversion, and to it we always come back, inasmuch as we make feeling the rule by which to judge of every good thing."

Epicurus then claims that there are two self-imposed beliefs that do the most to make our lives unhappy or full of pain. They are first, the belief that we will be punished by the gods for our bad actions, and second, that death is something to be feared. Both of these beliefs produce fear and anxiety, and are completely unnecessary since they are based on fictions. While the gods do indeed exist, being perfect and eternal they do not directly concern themselves with human affairs. As such, we have no need to fear any punishment from them, nor do we need to spend time in laborious acts of pious worship. As for death, he points out that once sentient experience comes to an end there will be no sensation of pain. As such, the fear of death is completely groundless. Indeed, he sounds curiously like a Zen master when he writes "Death is meaningless to the living because they are living, and meaningless to the dead... because they are dead."

Epicurus makes an important distinction between necessary and unnecessary desires. Necessary desires are those which are necessary to produce happiness, such as desiring to get rid of bodily pain, or desiring a state of inner tranquility. He writes that "the end of all our actions is to be free from pain and fear, and once this is obtained the tempest of the soul is quelled." Only when we are in pain do we feel the need to seek pleasure, a need which inevitably only produces greater pain. In order to get rid of this pain-pleasure-pain cycle, we need to cultivate a mindset in which there is no pain. Thus the aim is not the positive pursuit of pleasure, as it was for Aristippus. The aim is rather the attaining of a neutral state which is best described as "peace of mind" or even "emptiness," to use a Buddhist expression. The Greek word Epicurus uses for this state is **ataraxia**, which literally means "freedom from worry."

Epicurus notes further that we need wisdom to see which pleasures are really pleasurable, and which pains are necessary to produce pleasure. Some pleasures lead to greater pain, like imbibing copious amounts of alcohol, and so the wise person will shun them. On the other hand, certain pains, like sadness, can lead to an appreciation for life or compassion, which are highly pleasurable states. We should not therefore get rid of all negative emotions but only those that lead to unnecessary pains. This, by the way, is also one of the main conclusions that positive psychologist **Ed Diener** outlines in his latest research on the empirical basis of happiness.

Another one of the main conclusions of recent research on happiness concerns the limited role that external conditions play in making one happy. It has been found that income, marriage, good looks, even winning the lottery only have a small impact on one's lasting happiness. Epicurus anticipates this with his claim that the greatest secret to happiness is to be as independent of external things as possible. Being content with the simple things in life ensures that you will never be disappointed. If you put your stock in unnecessary pleasures like costly luxuries and food, you will be (1) upset when you lose these things, (2) anxious to obtain them, and (3) continually pushed onwards towards greater luxuries and hence greater anxiety and disappointment.

In keeping with this sentiment, Epicurus disparages the "crass hedonism" which emphasizes **physical pleasure**, and instead claims that the philosophical **pursuit of wisdom** with close friends is the greatest of pleasures; "When we say, then, that pleasure is the end and the aim, we do not mean the pleasures of the prodigal or the pleasures of sensuality, as we are understood to do through ignorance, prejudice, or wilful misrepresentation. By pleasure we mean the absence of pain in the body and trouble in the soul. It is not an unbroken succession of drinking bouts and of revelry, not sexual lust, not the enjoyment of fish and other delicacies of a luxurious table, that produces a pleasant life. It is rather sober reasoning, searching out the grounds of choice and avoidance, and banishing those beliefs that lead to the tumult of the soul."

Based on this conception of happiness, it is the philosopher who is the happiest of all people, for he chooses the stable pleasures of knowledge over the temporary and volatile pleasures of the body. Epicurus concludes his letter by saying that if one practices these precepts, he will become a "god among men," for he will have achieved an immortal state even whilst in a mortal body. As he writes: "Exercise yourself in these precepts day and night both by yourself and with one who is like minded; then never, either in waking or in one's dreams will you be disturbed, but will live as a god among men. For man loses all semblance of mortality by living in the midst of immortal blessings."

Note the emphasis Epicurus places on practicing the precepts "with one who is like minded." In keeping with Aristotle, Epicurus sees the indispensable value of friendship as a crucial motivator towards one's own true happiness. The problem is that more often than not, other people are a detriment to our happiness, by creating false competition for unnecessary pleasures. The solution to this is to remove oneself from ordinary society and to create a special commune where you interact only with those fellow like-minded pursuers of wisdom. In creating this vision, Epicurus no doubt influenced many **Utopian thinkers** from **Thomas More** to **Karl Marx** who pin their hopes of happiness on a complete change in the social relations that form the fabric of who we are as human beings.

The Epicurean Life

Epicurus placed an extremely high value on friendship. A saying with rather a more poetic flair than is Epicurus' custom runs: "Friendship goes dancing round the world, announcing to all of us to wake up to happiness". Epicurus held that a wise man would feel the torture of a friend no less than his own, and would die for a friend rather than betray him, for otherwise his own life would be confounded. These are powerfully **altruistic sentiments** for a philosopher who posits as the unique goal in life happiness based on freedom from physical pain and mental anxiety. Epicurus could justify such an attitude by the same prudential calculus that he uses to argue in favour of living justly: only by living in such a way that loyalty to friends is perceived to be a consummate value will one be able to feel secure in one's friends, and thus maximize one's felicity. Yet this does not seem quite what Epicurus means when he says that "friendship or love had its beginning as a result of utility, but is to be chosen for its own sake". The question is further complicated by the report in **Cicero's On Moral Ends** that there was a difference of opinion concerning friendship among later Epicureans. Since human beings were originally asocial and only later learned to form alliances and compacts, it is possible that Epicurus means to say that this capacity for friendship arose out of need, but that once the capacity for such feelings was acquired, feeling them came to be valued in itself. The argument would be similar to the modern idea that altruism could have developed as a result of natural selection. But the evidence does not permit a firm conclusion on this matter.

When Epicurus spoke of friendship, he may have had at least partly in mind specifically the relationship among his followers, who seem to have thought of themselves as friends. Epicureans were encouraged to form communities and to observe certain rituals, although most of these practices, such as the celebration each month of the day on which Epicurus was born or wearing rings bearing an image of Epicurus, may have originated after the founder's death.

The Epicureans paid attention to problems of pedagogy as well, laying out the best way to correct the ideas of people new to the school and its community without cajoling or discouraging them. It must be remembered that Epicurus understood the task of philosophy first and foremost as a form of **therapy for life**, since philosophy that does not heal the soul is no better than medicine that cannot cure the body. A life free of mental anxiety and open to the enjoyment of other pleasures was deemed equal to that of the gods. Indeed, it is from the gods themselves, via the simulacra that reach us from their abode, that we derive our image of blessed happiness, and prayer for the Epicureans consisted not in petitioning favours but rather in a receptivity to this vision. Although they held the gods to be immortal and indestructible, human pleasure might nevertheless equal divine, since pleasure, Epicurus maintained, is not augmented by duration; the **catastematic pleasure** experienced by a human being completely free of mental distress and with no bodily pain to disturb him or her is at the absolute top of the scale. Nor is such pleasure difficult to achieve: it is a mark precisely of those desires that are neither natural nor necessary that they are hard to satisfy. Epicurus was famously content with little, since on such a diet a small delicacy is as good as a feast, in addition to which it is easier to achieve self-sufficiency, and "the greatest benefit of self-sufficiency is freedom".

Epicureanism and Religion

Epicureanism emphasizes the neutrality of the gods and their non-interference with human lives, although it did not deny the existence of gods, despite some tendencies towards **Atheism**. It conceived of the gods as blissful and immortal, yet material, beings made of atoms, inhabiting the empty spaces between worlds in the vastness of infinite space, too far away from the earth to have any interest in what man was doing. It rejected any possibility of an afterlife, while still contending that one need not fear death. It can be argued that the philosophy is atheistic on a practical level, but avoids the charge of Atheism on the theoretical level, thus avoiding the fate of Socrates, who was tried and executed for the Atheism of his beliefs.

The Paradox of Epicurus is the earliest known description of the "Problem of evil", and is a famous argument against the existence of an all-powerful and providential God or gods. It can be stated: If God is willing to prevent evil, but is not able to, then He is not **omnipotent**; if He is able, but not willing, then He is **malevolent**; if He is both able and willing, then why is there such a thing as evil; and if He is neither able nor willing, then why call Him God at all? There are interesting parallels to **Buddhism**, which similarly emphasizes a lack of divine interference and has aspects of Atomism. Buddhism also resembles Epicureanism in its temperateness, including the belief that great excesses lead to great dissatisfaction.

Summary

The philosophy of Epicurus (341–270 B.C.E.) was a complete and interdependent system, involving a view of the goal of human life, an empiricist theory of knowledge, a description of nature based on atomistic materialism, and a naturalistic account of evolution, from the formation of the world to the emergence of human societies. Epicurus believed that, on the basis of a radical materialism which dispensed with transcendent entities such as the Platonic Ideas or Forms, he could disprove the possibility of the soul's survival after death, and hence the prospect of punishment in the afterlife. He regarded the unacknowledged fear of death and punishment as the primary cause of anxiety among human beings, and anxiety in turn as the source of extreme and irrational desires. The elimination of the fears and corresponding desires would leave people free to pursue the pleasures, both physical and mental, to which they are naturally drawn, and to enjoy the peace of mind that is consequent upon their regularly expected and achieved satisfaction. It remained to explain how irrational fears arose in the first place: hence the importance of an account of social evolution. Epicurus was aware that deeply ingrained habits of thought are not easily corrected, and thus he proposed various exercises to assist the novice. His system included advice on the proper attitude toward politics and the gods, the role of sex, marriage and friendship, reflections on the nature of various meteorological and planetary phenomena, about which it was best to keep an open mind in the absence of decisive verification, and explanations of such processes as **gravity** and **magnetism**, which posed considerable challenges to the ingenuity of the earlier atomists. Although the overall structure of Epicureanism was designed to hang together and to serve its principal ethical goals, there was room for a great deal of intriguing philosophical argument concerning every aspect of the system, from the speed of atoms in a void to the origin of optical illusions.

Model Questions

- Explain the Philosophy of Epicurus.
- Briefly narrate the origin of Epicureanism.
- Compare the ideas of Epicureanism and Buddhism.
- Narrate the perspective of Epicureanism towards religion?
- Critically analyse implications of Epicureanism in our day to day life.
- Do you think Epicureanism and Atheism are related? Justify.

References

1. Annas, Julia (ed.), and Raphael Woolf (trans.), 2001. Cicero: On Moral Ends, Cambridge: Cambridge University Press.
2. Arrighetti, Graziano, 1973. Epicuro Opere, 2nd edition, Turin: Einaudi. (Best edition available, with Italian translation.)
3. Bailey, Cyril B., 1926. Epicurus: The Extant Remains, Oxford: Clarendon Press. (Best edition in English.)
4. Bollack, Jean (ed.), 1985. Il pensiero del piacere: Epicuro, testi morali, commentari, Genoa: La Quercia.
5. De Lacy, Phillip Howard and Estelle Allen De Lacy, 1978. Philodemus On Methods of Inference, 2nd edition, Naples: Bibliopolis.
6. Delattre, Daniel and Jackie Pigeaud (eds.), 2010. Les epicuriens, Paris: Gallimard. (Very rich collection of texts in translation.)
7. Hammerstaedt, Jürgen, Pierre-Marie Morel, Refik Güremen (eds.), 2017. Diogenes of Oinoanda: Epicureanism and Philosophical Debates / Diogène d'Œnoanda: Épicurisme et Controverses, Leuven: Leuven University Press.
8. Hessler, Jan Erik, 2014. Epikur: Brief an Menoikeus, Basil. (Best commentary on this epistle.)
9. http://www.dictionary.com/browse/epicureanism
10. http://www.epicurus.net/
11. http://www.pursuit-of-happiness.org/history-of-happiness/epicurus/
12. http://www.veryshortintroductions.com/view/10.1093/actrade/9780199688326.001.0001/actrade-9780199688326

13. https://en.wikipedia.org/wiki/Epicureanism
14. https://global.oup.com/academic/product/epicureanism-a-very-short-introduction-9780199688326?cc=in&lang=en&
15. https://plato.stanford.edu/entries/epicurus/
16. https://www.britannica.com/topic/Epicureanism
17. https://www.philosophybasics.com/branch_epicureanism.html
18. https://www.philosophybasics.com/movements_epicureanism.html
19. https://www.youtube.com/watch?v=86J7Jprxtdc
20. https://www.youtube.com/watch?v=exm1O3n-9AA
21. Indelli, Giovanni and Voula Tsouna-McKirahan (eds.), 1995. [Philodemus]: [On Choices and Avoidances], Naples: Bibliopolis.
22. Leone, Giuliana, 1984. "Epicuro, 'Della natura,' libro XIV," Cronache Ercolanesi, 14: 17–107.
23. Long, A.A. and David Sedley, 1987. The Hellenistic Philosophers, 2 volumes, Cambridge: Cambridge University Press. (Excellent collection of sources, with Greek text in volume 2, arranged by topic.)
24. Millot, C., 1977. "Epicure 'De la nature' livre XV," Cronache Ercolanesi, 7: 9–39.
25. Obbink, Dirk, 1996. Philodemus De pietate, Oxford: Clarendon Press.
26. Sedley, David, 1973. "Epicurus, 'On Nature' Book XXVIII," Cronache Ercolanesi, 3: 5–83.
27. Smith, Martin Ferguson (ed.), 1993. Diogenes of Oenoanda: The Epicurean Inscription, Naples: Bibliopolis.
28. Stern, Jacob (trans.), 1996. Palaephatus: On Unbelievable Tales, Wauconda, IL : Bolchazy-Carducci Publishers.

Chapter - 14

Nicomachean Ethics

Introduction

The **Nicomachean Ethics** is the name normally given to Aristotle's best-known work on ethics. The work, which plays a pre-eminent role in defining Aristotelian ethics, consists of ten books, originally separate scrolls, and is understood to be based on notes from his lectures at the Lyceum. **Nicomachean Ethics** is a philosophical inquiry into the nature of the **good life** for a human being. **Aristotle** begins the work by positing that there exists some ultimate good toward which, in the final analysis, all human actions ultimately aim. The necessary characteristics of the ultimate good are that it is complete, final, self-sufficient and continuous. This good toward which all human actions implicitly or explicitly aim is happiness in Greek, "eudaimonia," which can also be translated as blessedness or living well, and which is not a static state of being but a type of activity.

To discover the nature of human happiness it is necessary to determine what the function of a human being is, for a person's happiness will consist in fulfilling the natural function toward which his being is directed. This natural function must be something which is specific to human beings, which is essential to being human. A person is primarily his intellect. While the spirited and desiring parts of the soul are also important, the rational part of the soul is what one can most properly consider a person's identity. The activity which only human beings can perform is intellectual; it is activity of the highest part of the soul according to reason. **Human happiness**, therefore, consists in activity of the soul according to **reason**. In practical terms, this activity is expressed through ethical virtue, when a person directs his actions according to reason. The very highest human life, however, consists in contemplation of the greatest goods. More will be said later on this topic, which is the culmination of the Ethics.

Ethical virtue "is a habit disposed toward action by deliberate choice, being at the mean relative to us, and defined by reason as a prudent man would define it." Each of the elements of this definition is important. Virtue is not simply an isolated action but a habit of acting well. For an action to be virtuous a person must do it deliberately, knowing what he is doing, and doing it because it is a noble action. In each specific situation, the virtuous action is a mean between two extremes. Finally, prudence is necessary for ethical virtue because it is the intellectual virtue by which a person is able to determine the mean specific to each situation.

The first virtue discussed is bravery. It is a mean between rashness and cowardice. A brave man is one who faces and fears what he should for the right reason, in the right manner and at the right time. A brave man performs his actions for the sake of what is noble. A brave man is thus one who is fearless in facing a noble death.

The next virtue is **temperance**. It is a mean with regard to bodily pleasures. The intemperate man desires pleasurable things and chooses them because they are pleasurable; he is pained when he fails to get what he desires. A **temperate man** is moderately disposed with regard to pleasures and pains. He loves such pleasures as right reason dictates. Temperance keeps the desiring part of the soul in harmony with reason.

Generosity is the third virtue which Aristotle examines. With regard to property, generosity is a mean between wastefulness and stinginess. A generous man will give to the right person, the right amounts and at the right times. He will also take proper care of his possessions. Generosity does not depend on the quantity of the giving but on the habit of the giver, which takes into account the amount which the giver himself has and is able to give away.

The next virtue is **munificence**, which consists giving large amounts for suitable occasions. The deficiency of this virtue is called meanness and the excess is ostentation. A munificent man spends gladly and lavishly, not calculating costs, but always for a noble purpose.

Magnanimity, the fifth virtue Aristotle discusses, is one of the peaks of virtue. A magnanimous man claims and deserves great honours. Someone who deserves honours but doesn't claim them is low-minded, and someone who claims honours but does not deserve them is vain. It is better to be vain than low-minded, because vanity will be naturally corrected by life experience. A magnanimous man is great in each of the virtues, and is a sort of ornament of virtues because he shows how good a virtuous life is.

The next virtue concerns honour, specifically small and medium honours. It is a mean between too much and too little ambition which can be described as right ambition.

The virtue that is a mean with respect to anger is good temper. The excesses are irascibility or bitterness. If one is irascible he gets angry quickly and retaliates but then forgets about it. Someone who is bitter holds anger for a long time. A good tempered man is one who becomes angry on the right occasions, with the right people, at the right time and for the right length of time.

The next three virtues are **friendliness**, the mean between flattery or obsequiousness and quarrelsomeness; truthfulness, the mean between boastfulness and self-depreciation, and wit, the mean with regard to **humour** and **amusement**. Wit entails saying the right things in the right manner and also listening to things properly.

The last virtue, which unites and orders all of the other virtues, is **justice**. Justice can also be considered in a more specific sense, as one of the virtues. Both justice in the specific sense and justice as the whole of virtue are defined in relation to other people, but justice in the specific sense is concerned with honour, property, safety and similar things, while justice in the larger sense is concerned with virtue as a whole. Another subset of justice is distributive justice. Justice is a mean between two extremes of unfairness. What is just in distribution should be in some way according to merit, but not all agree what that merit should be. Advocates of mob rule say that this merit is freedom, oligarchs say that it is wealth, others say that it is good ancestry and aristocrats say that is virtue.

Prudence is the intellectual virtue of practical reason. It is concerned with human actions and gives a person the ability to choose what the virtuous mean is in specific situations. Acquiring prudence requires time and experience. **Prudence** and **ethical virtue** are both necessary for one another.

Friendship is a necessary part of the good life. There are three types of friendship: friendship based on **usefulness**, friendship based on **pleasure** and friendship based on **virtue**. Only the last type is genuine friendship. Friendships based on usefulness and pleasure tend not to be very enduring, since they only last as the long as each party derives the usefulness or pleasure he desires from the relationship. Friendship based on virtue is based on wishing the good for the other person. This genuine friendship is necessary for self-knowledge and helps both of the friends to grow in virtue. Friendship presupposes justice and goes beyond it. The virtue of a friend is to love. The relationship one has with a friend is like the harmonious relationship between the different parts of the soul of a virtuous man.

Man's highest action and most complete happiness is a life of contemplation of the highest goods. Man's intellectual capacity is his highest capacity, and therefore his highest happiness resides in the use of that capacity. The life of contemplation is so sublime that it is practically divine, and man can achieve it only insofar as there is something divine in him. Contemplation is the action which best fulfils all the qualifications that the ultimate good should have, because it is the most continuous, complete and self-sufficient of all actions.

For most people, mere exhortation will not be enough to make them act virtuously. Consequently, good laws are necessary in order to make people virtuous. Laws and proper education are necessarily especially for the young, in order to train their passions and desires to be in accord with reason. Yet since such a great number of men are not virtuous, laws are necessary not just for the young, but for everyone.

Historical Context

Aristotle was born at **Stagira** in northern Greece in 384 B.C. His father, **Nicomachus**, was a physician at the court of **Philip of Macedon**, the father of **Alexander the Great**. In BC 367, Aristotle moved to **Athens**, which was the intellectual and cultural centre of ancient **Greece**. He spent many years studying in **Plato's Academy**, surrounded by other philosophers, scientists, and mathematicians. Plato died in 347, and Aristotle left the Academy in that same year. There is speculation that he left because Plato had not chosen him as his successor. It is more likely, however, that anti-Macedonian sentiment was growing in Athens, and Aristotle was afraid of being persecuted for his associations with **King Philip**'s court.

Over the next four years, Aristotle travelled throughout the **Eastern Aegean** area, studying and teaching. During this time, he conducted a remarkable array of experiments and observations in the **Biological Sciences**. In 343, he was summoned back north to **Macedonia** to be the personal tutor to the young **Alexander the Great**. While we know very little about Aristotle's influence on Alexander, there has been a great deal of speculation and mythologizing about the relationship between these two eminent figures.

As the Macedonians extended their empire over Greece, it became safe for Aristotle to return to Athens. In 334, he established his own philosophical school at the **Lyceum**, where he taught for the next eleven years. His lectures covered almost every area of study, including physics, metaphysics, ethics, psychology, politics, and poetry. His pioneering work in logic and biology was not improved upon for two thousand years.

In 323, Alexander the Great died, and Aristotle left Athens, fearing another upsurge of anti-Macedonian sentiment. Alluding to the trial and execution of Socrates some seventy-six years earlier, Aristotle reportedly claimed that he did not wish the Athenians to "sin a second time against philosophy." A year later, he died in Chalcis in Euboea.

Though Aristotle published many admired works in his lifetime, none have survived to the present day. Those works that we do have consist mostly of lecture notes from his courses at the Lyceum. That these works were never intended for publication explains why they are generally dry and hard to follow. *The Nicomachean Ethics* was likely either edited by or dedicated to Aristotle's son, **Nicomachus**.

The Greek world of Aristotle's time was made up of small city-states, each with its own autonomous government. The city-state consisted of slaves, noncitizen manual labourers, children, women, aliens, and citizens. The citizens were adult males, most of whom had been born to citizen parents. The citizens governed the city, while the slaves, labourers, and women did all the work to provide the necessary food, shelter, and equipment. Because they were freed from the necessity of meeting day-to-day needs, citizens enjoyed a great deal of freedom and luxury. The leisure they enjoyed was highly valued and made possible one of the greatest periods of intellectual energy in human history. That this system was exploitative is hardly debatable, but it also produced an incredible array of philosophy, drama, art, and architecture. Aristotle's students were young citizens whose tuition was meant to prepare them for a life of civic duty.

There were few enough citizens that everyone in a given city would at least recognize, if not know, one another, and all citizens were expected to take part in public office. Unlike our modern system of representative democracy, where we simply elect officials to speak for us, all Greek citizens were expected to voice their own opinions in large deliberative and judicial assemblies. There was a strong bond of kinship created in citizenship, as the same people lived together, governed together, served in the army together, and enjoyed leisure time together.

The age of the city-state came to a close within Aristotle's lifetime, however, due to the efforts of his most famous pupil, Alexander the Great. Alexander came to power in the northern kingdom of Macedonia and within a decade had established one of the largest empires the world has ever seen. When Alexander died, Greece once more became fragmented, but the fierce independence of the city-states was a thing of the past. Greek culture was on the decline, and within a few hundred years, it would be swallowed up by the burgeoning Roman Empire.

Philosophical Context

As the successor of **Socrates** and **Plato**, **Aristotle** was the last of the great Greek philosophers. Philosophy first flourished in Greece sometime in the early sixth century B.C. as inquisitive thinkers began developing rational methods for investigating the mysteries of nature and mathematics. These pre-Socratic thinkers were as much scientists and mathematicians as they were philosophers.

While there is significant pre-Socratic influence in Aristotle's work, primarily in the sciences and metaphysics, his most significant influence was undoubtedly Plato (427–347 B.C.). Plato's philosophy was centred on his famous **Theory of Forms**, or **Theory of Ideas**. The theory is based on the observation that there must be some universal quality that all things classed under a single name share in common. For instance, a flower is beautiful in a very different way from a human, but both the flower and the human must share something in common if we are to call them both "beautiful." Plato's answer is that they share in common the "Form of Beauty," which is itself invisible, unchanging, and eternal. Anything that we perceive in this world as beautiful is beautiful because it participates in some way in the Form of Beauty. But while beautiful flowers will wilt and beautiful humans will grow old and die, the Form of Beauty is everlasting and unchanging. Plato theorizes that our world of sensible experience, with its changes and disappointments, is but a poor reflection of the ideal world of pure Forms that underlies our experience. The goal of philosophy, then, is to train the mind to see beyond the veil of experience and to contemplate the true reality of Forms that lies behind it.

While Aristotle was undoubtedly influenced by Plato, this influence was mostly negative. Most of his works, including the Nicomachean Ethics, contain involved refutations of many of Plato's theories. Aristotle himself was an empirical scientist who felt that true wisdom comes from examining the objects of experience and not from trying to look beyond them. In the Ethics, he is primarily critical of Plato's Form of Good. According to Aristotle, there is not a single Form by virtue of which all good things are good. Instead, he discusses at length the multiplicity of the various virtues.

Aristotle's work in the Ethics is deeply informed by his own work in the **Sciences** and **Metaphysics**. In terms of impact on the Ethics, Aristotle's most significant concept is that of the **teleology of nature**. According to Aristotle, nature works toward a telos, or end goal. His biological work aims constantly at the question of what purpose different aspects of plants and animals serve. He classifies humans as "rational animals," meaning that our telos is rational. In other words, our function in life is to realize our full potential as rational beings. If we are not fully rational, we are falling short of our true nature.

This teleological view gives Aristotle's Ethics a clear sense of direction. Our goal in life is to achieve our true nature, and this true nature consists essentially of rationality. The purpose of a moral education, then, is to teach us how we may become perfectly rational and immune to the temptations of our lower animalistic parts.

Ethics is just one of a number of fields that Aristotle classifies as "practical science." Unlike the natural sciences, which examine the world around us, these sciences deal with the practical aspects of human society and how best to arrange this society. The practical sciences are all closely connected, and Aristotle frequently expounds on the connection between the good life for the individual and the kind of state that could make this good life possible. Hence, Aristotle's Politics is an important companion and sequel to his Ethics.

While the Nicomachean Ethics is Aristotle's most popular work on ethics, there is a second work called the **Eudemian Ethics**, which is far less widely read. Most scholars agree that the Eudemian Ethics was written earlier in Aristotle's career and represents a less mature view. Books V, VI, and VII of the Nicomachean Ethics are also found in the Eudemian Ethics.

Aristotle's influence on Western philosophy is difficult to exaggerate. While his works were lost to the West for many centuries, they were slowly transmitted back into Europe by Arab scholars during the Middle Ages. Thanks mostly to the influence of **Saint Thomas Aquinas**, Aristotelian philosophy became accepted almost as dogmatically as the Bible during the late Middle Ages. While modern philosophy broke significantly from the scholastic tradition of the Middle Ages, Aristotle's influence remains undiminished. In particular, his emphasis on scientific reasoning and experimentation has been a cornerstone of modern empiricist philosophy.

Summary

The Nicomachean is the name normally given to Aristotle's best-known work on ethics. The work, which plays a pre-eminent role in defining Aristotelian ethics, consists of ten books, originally separate scrolls, and is understood to be based on notes from his lectures at the Lyceum. The title is often assumed to refer to his son **Nicomachus**, to whom the work was dedicated or who may have edited it. Alternatively, the work may have been dedicated to his father, who was also called Nicomachus. The theme of the work is a Socratic question previously explored in the works of Plato, Aristotle's friend and teacher, of how men should best live. In his Metaphysics, Aristotle described how Socrates, the friend and teacher of Plato, had turned philosophy to human questions, whereas pre-Socratic philosophy had only been theoretical. Ethics, as now separated out for discussion by Aristotle, is practical rather than theoretical, in the original Aristotelian senses of these terms. In other words, it is not only a contemplation about good living, because it also aims to create good living. It is therefore connected to Aristotle's other practical work, the Politics, which similarly aims at people becoming good. Ethics is about how individuals should best live, while the study of politics is from the perspective of a law-giver, looking at the good of a whole community.

Model Questions

- Explain the Philosophy of Aristotle on Virtue.
- Briefly narrate the origin and development of Nicomachean Ethics.
- Compare the ideas of Aristotle with on Friendship.

- Narrate three types of Friendship according to Nicomachean Ethics.
- Critically analyse implications of Nicomachean Ethics in our day to day life.
- How Nicomachean Ethics and Eudemian Ethics differ?

References

1. Bostock, David (2000). Aristotle's Ethics. New York: Oxford University Press.
2. Broadie, Sarah (1991). Ethics with Aristotle. New York: Oxford University Press.
3. Burger, Ronna (2008). Aristotle's Dialogue with Socrates: On the Nicomachean Ethics. University of Chicago Press.
4. Cooper, John M. (1975). Reason and Human Good in Aristotle. Cambridge: Harvard University Press.
5. Hardie, W.F.R. (1968). Aristotle's Ethical Theory. Oxford: Oxford University Press.
6. Hughes, Gerald J. (2001). Routledge Philosophy Guidebook to Aristotle on Ethics. London: Routledge.
7. Kraut, Richard (1989). Aristotle on the Human Good. Princeton: Princeton University Press.
8. Kraut, ed., Richard (2006). The Blackwell Guide to Aristotle's Nicomachean Ethics. Oxford: Blackwell.
9. May, Hope (2010). Aristotle's Ethics Moral Development and Human Nature. London: Continuum.
10. Pakaluk, Michael (2005). Aristotle's Nicomachean Ethics: An Introduction. Chicago: University of Chicago Press.
11. Rorty, ed., Amelie (1980). Essays on Aristotle's Ethics. Berkeley: University of California Press.
12. Reeve, C.D.C. (1992). Practices of Reason: Aristotle's Nicomachean Ethics. New York: Oxford University Press.
13. Pangle, Lorraine (2003). Aristotle and the Philosophy of Friendship. New York: Cambridge University Press.
14. Sherman, ed., Nancy (1999). Aristotle's Ethics: Critical Essays. New York: Rowman & Littlefield.
15. Urmson, J.O. (1988). Aristotle's Ethics. New York: Blackwell.
16. Warne, Christopher (2007). Aristotle's Nicomachean Ethics: Reader's Guide. London: Continuum.
17. https://en.wikipedia.org/wiki/Nicomachean_Ethics
18. http://www.sparknotes.com/philosophy/ethics/context/
19. http://www.sparknotes.com/philosophy/ethics/section1/
20. http://classics.mit.edu/Aristotle/nicomachaen.html
21. https://socialsciences.mcmaster.ca/econ/ugcm/3ll3/aristotle/Ethics.pdf

22. http://oll.libertyfund.org/titles/aristotle-the-nicomachean-ethics
23. https://www.shmoop.com/nicomachean-ethics/
24. https://www.gradesaver.com/aristotles-ethics/study-guide/summary
25. http://www.constitution.org/ari/ethic_00.htm

Chapter - 15

Concept of the Soul

Introduction

Among Western philosophers, the ancient Greeks provided much insight into the nature of the soul. Two paradigmatic viewpoints were articulated by the philosophers Plato and Aristotle. Plato, drawing on the words of his teacher **Socrates**, considered the soul as the essence of a person, which is an incorporeal, eternal occupant of our being. As our bodies die the soul is continually reborn in subsequent bodies. For **Plato**, the soul comprises three parts, each having a function in a balanced and peaceful life:

- the **logos** (superego, mind, nous, or reason). The logos corresponds to the charioteer, directing the balanced horses of appetite and spirit. It allows for logic to prevail, and for the optimisation of balance.
- the **thymos** (emotion, ego, or spiritedness). The thymos comprises our emotional motive (ego), that which drives us to acts of bravery and glory. If left unchecked, it leads to hubris - the most fatal of all flaws in the Greek view.
- the **pathos** (appetitive, id, or carnal). The pathos equates to the appetite (id) that drives humankind to seek out its basic bodily needs. When the passion controls us, it drives us to hedonism in all forms. In the Ancient Greek view, this is the basal and most feral state.

Although Aristotle agreed with Plato that the soul is the core essence of a being, he argued against its having a separate existence. Unlike Plato, Aristotle did not consider the soul as some kind of separate, ghostly occupant of the body. According to him, the soul is an actuality of a living body, and thus it cannot be immortal. Aristotle describes this concept of the soul in many of his works such as the De Anima. He believed that there were four parts, or powers, of the soul: the calculative part, the scientific part on the rational side used for making decisions and the desiderative part and the vegetative part on the irrational side responsible for identifying our needs.

Pre-Pythagorean belief was that the soul had no life when it departed from the body, and retired into Hades with no hope of returning to a body.

The main precursor of the modern concept of mind is the ancient Greek notion of soul (**psyche**), which was originally used to mark the difference between things that are alive and things that are dead. Conceptually, it was related to breath (pneuma), and was thought to come in degrees corresponding to different states of consciousness. Thus, a dead man was said to have lost his psyche entirely, whereas a sleeping or fainting man has lost enough of it to lose consciousness, though that too would bring him a step closer to death. The soul is composed of extremely light and tenuous matter, variously identified with pure and "breathable" elements such as air (as by the philosophers **Thales** [c. 625–c. 547 B.C.E] and **Anaximenes** [570–500? B.C.E.]) or fire by **Heraclitus** [c. 540–480 B.C.E.]). Most pre-Socratic thinkers would have understood the expression "he breathed his last" literally, and seen the dying gasps of a Homeric warrior, say, as the exhalation of his soul. If psyche could exist in a disembodied state - and it is doubtful whether most early Greek philosophers thought that it could - it would have been as a shadowy or ephemeral form, like the denizens of Hades.

With **Plato** (c. 428–348 or 347 B.C.E.), philosophers began to ask more sophisticated questions about how one can feel, think, possess knowledge, and choose rightly. Plato's strategy here was to divide the soul in terms of its capacities, producing the first faculty psychology in the western tradition.

In his earlier writings, Plato came closer than any other ancient or medieval philosopher to advancing a dualist account like that of **Descartes**. In the **Phaedo**, he took immortality to be an essential feature of the soul, so that "mortal soul" is a contradiction in terms. Thus, "when death comes to a man, the mortal part of him dies, but the immortal part retires at the approach of death and escapes unharmed and indestructible". But a soul immortal by definition has more in common with what is cosmic and divine than with anything in the visible realm - such as its own body, for example - which is why Plato shows little interest in exploring its everyday operations. The soul's union with the body is not its natural state; in fact, the whole point of philosophy is to prepare the soul for its release from the "prison" of the body.

Plato and Aristotle on Soul

Plato is more forthcoming in his later works, where the concept of the soul plays a major role in his explanation of moral conflict and human action. From the fact that one can be affected by two or more desires simultaneously, he infers that the soul cannot be unitary, since it is impossible for the same thing to act in opposite ways at the same time. Accordingly, in the Republic he identifies three distinct parts of the soul - reason (nous), passion (thumos), and appetite (epithumia) - and posits these as the source of conflicting desires. Reason rules over the soul with wisdom, but opposed to it is appetite, the irrational part of the soul "with which it loves, hungers, thirsts, and feels the flutter and titillation of other desires". Reason and appetite would remain in unending combat but for the intervention of passion, the "spirited" part of the soul that helps reason subdue appetite. Plato has in mind here the experience of steeling our resolve, when we angrily force ourselves to do something we don't want to do because reason has judged it to be the best course of action. What is important about this model, however, is the elevation of rationality to the dominant position in the soul, and conversely, the denigration of appetite as an irrational force that threatens to destroy our well-being. In the **Phaedrus**, Plato likens reason to a charioteer trying to control two horses: a good horse (passion), who "needs no whip" because he is driven by the command of reason alone, and a bad horse (appetite), who is hard to control and who would run the chariot into the ditch if left unchecked. Plato saw no redeeming value for the emotions in human moral life, though anger, at least, could sometimes be placed in the service of reason.

Aristotle (384–322 B.C.E.) took the study of the soul in a less speculative direction. He wrote an entire treatise on the soul that views the soul as a natural phenomenon. The soul is defined as "an actuality of the first kind of a natural organized body": that which makes the body alive and capable of performing its characteristic functions. Aristotle divides these into vegetative powers, concerned with nutrition and growth; sensory powers; and intellectual powers. In his broader taxonomy of life forms, these correspond to the souls of plants, brute animals, and human beings, respectively, with the higher forms subsuming the powers of those lower in the hierarchy. Only the third capacity is relevant to the modern conception of mind, though it should be noted that this is far from being a dualist conception. Aristotle's intellect is a perfection of the organic unity of body and soul, and although he concedes that the activity of thinking is "separable, impassible, and unmixed", thinking cannot occur without sensory images.

The Greek Notion of Soul

The **Homeric** poems, with which most ancient writers can safely be assumed to be intimately familiar, use the word 'soul' in two distinguishable, probably related, ways. The soul is, on the one hand, something that a human being risks in battle and loses in death. On the other hand, it is what at the time of death departs from the person's limbs and travels to the underworld, where it has a more or less pitiful afterlife as a shade or image of the deceased person. It has been suggested that what is referred to as soul in either case is in fact thought of as one and the same thing, something that a person can risk and lose and that, after death, endures as a shade in the underworld. The suggestion is plausible, but cannot be verified. In any case, once a person's soul has departed for good, the person is dead. The presence of soul therefore distinguishes a living human body from a corpse. However, this is plainly not to say that the soul is thought of as what accounts for, or is responsible for, the activities, responses, operations and the like that constitute a person's life. Homer never says that anyone does anything in virtue of, or with, their soul, nor does he attribute any activity to the soul of a living person. Thus, though the presence or absence of soul marks out a person's life, it is not otherwise associated with that life. Moreover, it is a striking feature of Homeric usage that, in Furley's words, to mention soul is to suggest death: someone's soul comes to mind only when their life is thought, by themselves or others, to be at risk. Thus **Achilles** says that he is continuously risking his soul, and **Agenor** reflects on the fact that even Achilles has just one soul. It should also be pointed out that in the Homeric poems, only human beings are said to have souls. Correspondingly, Homer never envisages shades or images of non-human creatures in the underworld. These two facts taken together suggest that in whatever precise way the soul is conceived of as associated with life, it is in any case thought to be connected not with life in general, or life in all its forms, but rather, more specifically, with the life of a human being.

Several significant developments occurred in the ways Greeks thought and spoke about the soul in the sixth and fifth centuries. The questions about the soul that are formulated and discussed in the writings of **Plato** and **Aristotle** to some extent arise from, and need to be interpreted against the background of, these sixth and fifth century developments. One factor that is of central importance is the gradual loss of the Homeric connection between mentioning a person's soul and the thought that their life is vulnerable or at risk. In ordinary fifth century Greek, having soul is simply being alive; hence the emergence, at about this time, of the adjective 'ensouled' as the standard word meaning "alive", which was applied not just to human beings, but to other living things as well. There is some reason to think that the word 'soul' was used in this straightforwardly positive way already in the sixth century. **Thales of Miletus**, who is credited with successfully predicting a solar eclipse occurring in 585 B.C., reportedly attributed soul to magnets, on the grounds that magnets are capable of moving iron. Thales' thought was presumably that since it is distinctive of living things to be able to initiate movement, magnets must in fact be alive or, in other words, ensouled. Thus, while Homer spoke of soul only in the case of human beings, in sixth and fifth century usage soul is attributed to every kind of living thing. What is in place, then, at this time is the notion that soul is what distinguishes that which is alive from that which is not.

However, it is not just that soul is said to be present in every living thing. It is also the case that an increasingly broad range of ways of acting and being acted on is attributed to the soul. Thus it has come to be natural, by the end of the fifth century, to refer pleasure taken in food and drink, as well as sexual desire, to the soul. People are said, for example, to satisfy their souls with rich food, and the souls of gods and men are claimed to be subject to sexual desire. In contexts of intense emotion or crisis, feelings like love and hate, joy and grief, anger and shame are associated with the soul.

Oedipus says that his soul laments the misery of his city and its inhabitants. Moreover, the soul is also importantly connected with boldness and courage, especially in battle. Courageous people are said, for instance in Herodotus and Thucydides, to have enduring or strong souls. In the **Hippocratic** text Airs, Waters, Places, the soul is thought of as the place of courage or, as the case may be, its opposite: in the case of lowland inhabitants, courage and endurance are not in their souls by nature, but must be instilled by law; similarly in benign climates, men are fleshy, ill-jointed, moist, without endurance and weak in soul.

The connection between the soul and characteristics like boldness and courage in battle is plainly an aspect of the noteworthy fifth century development whereby the soul comes to be thought of as the source or bearer of moral qualities such as, for instance, temperance and justice. In Pericles' funeral oration that **Thucydides** includes in his account of the Peloponnesian War, he says that those who know most clearly the sweet and the terrible, and yet do not as a result turn away from danger, are rightly judged "strongest with regard to soul". This text, and others like it, indicate a semantic extension whereby 'soul' comes to denote a person's moral character, often, but not always, with special regard to qualities such as endurance and courage. While the connection with courage is obvious in a number of texts, there are other texts in which the soul is the bearer of other admirable qualities, such as a Euripidean fragment that speaks of the desire characteristic of a soul that is just, temperate and good. Hippolytus, in Euripides' play named after him, describes himself as having a "virgin soul", obviously to evoke his abstinence from sex. In Pindar's second Olympian, salvation is promised to those who "keep their souls from unjust acts". The last two texts mentioned may well be influenced by Orphic and Pythagorean beliefs about the nature and immortality of the soul, to which we will turn in due course. But it would be a mistake to think that the moralization of the soul wholly depended on Orphic and Pythagorean speculation. It would, at the very least, be to disregard the soul's connection with courage in poetry, the historians and in Hippocratic writings.

The 5th Century Greek Notion of Soul

To educated fifth century speakers of Greek, it would have been natural to think of qualities of soul as accounting for, and being manifested in, a person's morally significant behaviour. **Pericles** acts courageously, and **Hippolytus** temperately, because of the qualities of their souls from which such actions have a strong tendency to flow, and their actions express and make evident the courage, temperance and the like that characterize their souls. Once we are in a position properly to appreciate the connection between soul and moral character that must already have been felt to be natural at this stage, it should come as no surprise that the soul is also taken to be something that engages in activities like thinking and planning. If the soul is, in some sense, responsible for courageous acts, for instance, it is only to be expected that the soul also grasps what, in the circumstances, courage calls for, and how, at some suitable level of detail, the courageous act must be performed. Thus in a speech of Antiphon, the jury is urged to "take away from the accused the soul that planned the crime", in striking **juxtaposition** of the ideas of life-soul and of soul as responsible for practical thought. Somewhat similarly, in a Sophoclean fragment someone says that "a kindly soul with just thoughts is a better inventor than any sophist". Moreover, it is easy to see that there are connections between familiar uses of 'soul' in emotional contexts and attributions to the soul of cognitive and intellectual activities and achievements. There is, after all, no clear-cut and manifest difference between, say, being in the emotional state of fear and having a terrifying thought or perception. When Oedipus' soul laments, or Ajax's soul is bitten by dishonour, emotion obviously goes hand in hand with cognition, and if it is natural to refer the one to the soul, there should be nothing puzzling about attributions to it of the other. Thus in non-philosophical Greek of the fifth century the soul is treated as the bearer of moral qualities, and also as responsible for practical thought and cognition.

From Homer to the end of the fifth century, the word 'soul' undergoes remarkable semantic expansion, in the course of which it comes to be natural not only to speak of soul as what distinguishes the living from the dead and the animate from the inanimate, but also to attribute to the soul a wide variety of activities and responses, cognitive as well as emotional, and to think of it as the bearer of such virtues as courage, temperance and justice. As a result of these developments, the language made available something that Homeric Greek lacked, a distinction between body and soul. Thus the Hippocratic author of Airs, Waters, Places writes of "endurance in body and soul". **Antiphon** says of a defendant who is sure of his innocence that though his body may surrender, his soul saves him by its willingness to struggle, through knowledge of its innocence. For the guilty, on the other hand, even a strong body is to no avail, since his soul fails him, "believing the vengeance coming to him is for his impieties". Homer, by contrast, knows and speaks of a whole lot of different sources and bearers of psychological predicates, but lacks a word to pick out the soul as a single item to which the predicates in question can, in some way or other, be referred and which can be distinguished from, and in suitable contexts contrasted with, the body.

Summary

Ancient philosophy did not, of course, end with classical Stoicism, or indeed with the Hellenistic period, and neither did ancient theorizing about the soul. The revival of interest in the works of both **Plato** and **Aristotle** beginning in the second half of the second century B.C. prominently included renewed interest in Platonic and

Aristotelian conceptions of the soul, sparking novel theoretical developments, such as, for instance, Plotinus' argument that the soul could not be spatially extended, since no spatially extended item could account for the unity of the subject of sense-perception. Christian writers such as **Clement of Alexandria** and **Gregory of Nyssa** were heavily indebted to philosophical theories of soul, especially Platonic ones, but also introduced new concerns and interests of their own. Nevertheless, these and other post-classical developments in every case need to be interpreted within the framework and context furnished by the classical theories that we have been considering in some detail.

Model Questions

1. Write a short note on Concept of Soul.
2. Narrate the ideas of Plato and Aristotle on Soul.
3. Write a short note on the 5th century notion on Soul.
4. What is the Pre-Pythagorean belief on soul?
5. For Plato, the soul comprises three parts. Which are they?
6. How Homeric poems perceive on Concept of Soul.

References

1. Algra, K., J. Barnes, J. Mansfeld & M. Schofield, (eds.), 1999, The Cambridge History of Hellenistic Philosophy, Cambridge: Cambridge University Press.
2. Annas, J. E., 1992, Hellenistic Philosophy of Mind, Berkeley: University of California Press.
3. Barnes, J., (ed.), 1984, The Complete Works of Aristotle, Princeton: Princeton University Press.
4. Cooper, J. M. & D. S. Hutchinson, (eds.), 1997, Plato: Complete Works, Indianapolis: Hackett.
5. Cooper, J. M., 1999, Reason and Emotion, Princeton: Princeton University Press.
6. Everson, S., (ed.), 1991, Companions to Ancient Thought 2: Psychology, Cambridge: Cambridge University Press.
7. http://science.jrank.org/pages/10723/Philosophy-Mind-Ancient-Medieval-Ancient-Greek-Roman-Views.html
8. http://www.cambridgescholars.com/download/sample/60735
9. http://www.metanexus.net/essay/holistic-concepts-soul-ancient-mediterranean-world

10. http://www.mountainrunnerdoc.com/greekviewsonthesoul.html
11. http://www.newworldencyclopedia.org/entry/Soul
12. https://en.wikipedia.org/wiki/Soul
13. https://plato.stanford.edu/entries/ancient-soul/
14. https://www.britannica.com/topic/soul-religion-and-philosophy
15. https://www.encyclopedia.com/environment/encyclopedias-almanacs-transcripts-and-maps/soul-greek-and-hellenistic-concepts
16. https://www.speakingtree.in/allslides/nature-journey-of-soul
17. Kirk, G. S., J. E. Raven & M. Schofield, (eds.), 1983, The Presocratic Philosophers, Cambridge: Cambridge University Press. [=KR&S]
18. Long, A. A. & D. N. Sedley, (eds.), 1987, The Hellenistic Philosophers, Cambridge: Cambridge University Press. [=L&S]
19. Lorenz, H., 2006, The Brute Within, Oxford: Oxford University Press.
20. Price, A. W., 1995, Mental Conflict, London: Routledge.
21. Smith, M. F., 1993, Diogenes of Oenoanda: The Epicurean Inscription, La Scuola di Epicuro, Suppl. 1, Naples: Bibliopolis.

Chapter - 16

The Process of Change: The Four Causes

Introduction

The "**four causes**" are elements of an influential principle in Aristotelian thought whereby explanations of change or movement are classified into four fundamental types of answer to the question "why?". Aristotle wrote that "we do not have knowledge of a thing until we have grasped its why, that is to say, its cause." While there are cases where identifying a "cause" is difficult, or in which "causes" might merge, Aristotle held that his four "causes" provided an analytical scheme of general applicability.

Aitia, from Greek word that Aristotle used to refer to the causal explanation that has traditionally been translated as "**cause**", but this specialized, technical, philosophical usage of the word "cause" does not correspond exactly to its most usual applications in everyday English language. The translation of Aristotle's ***Aitia*** that is nearest to current ordinary language could be "**question**" or "**causal explanation**", although any such terms may mask the fact that Aristotelians consider the four causes to be more fundamental in nature than mere explanations. Aristotle held that there were four kinds of answers to "why" questions. They are:

- **Matter**: a change or movement's material cause, is the aspect of the change or movement which is determined by the material that composes the moving or changing things. For a table, that might be wood; for a statue, that might be bronze or marble.

- **Form**: a change or movement's formal cause, is a change or movement caused by the arrangement, shape or appearance of the thing changing or moving. Aristotle says for example that the ratio 2:1, and number in general, is the cause of the octave.
- **Agent**: a change or movement's efficient or moving cause, consists of things apart from the thing being changed or moved, which interact so as to be an agency of the change or movement. For example, the efficient cause of a table is a carpenter, or a person working as one, and according to Aristotle the efficient cause of a boy is a father.
- **End or purpose**: a change or movement's final cause, is that for the sake of which a thing is what it is. For a seed, it might be an adult plant. For a sailboat, it might be sailing. For a ball at the top of a ramp, it might be coming to rest at the bottom.

The four "causes" are not mutually exclusive. For Aristotle, several answers to the question "why" have to be given to explain a phenomenon and especially the actual configuration of an object. For example, if asking why a table is such and such, a complete explanation, taking into account the four causes, would sound like this: This table is solid and brown because it is made of wood (matter), it does not collapse because it has four legs of equal length (form), it is as such because a carpenter made it starting from a tree (agent), it has these dimensions because it is to be used by men and women (end).

In his philosophical writings, Aristotle used the Greek word ***aition***, a neuter singular form of an adjective. The Greek word had meant, perhaps originally in a "legal" context, what or who is "responsible", mostly but not always in a bad sense of "guilt" or "blame"; alternatively it could mean "to the credit of" someone or something. The appropriation of this word by Aristotle and other philosophers reflects how the Greek experience of legal practice influenced the concern in Greek thought to determine what is responsible. The word developed other meanings, including its use in philosophy in a more abstract sense. About a century before Aristotle, the anonymous author of the **Hippocratic** text On Ancient Medicine had described the essential characteristics of a cause: "We must, therefore, consider the causes of each [medical] condition to be those things which are such that, when they are present, the condition necessarily occurs, but when they change to another combination, it ceases." In the present context, Aristotle used the four causes to provide different answers to the question, "because of what?" The four answers to this question illuminate different aspects of how a thing comes into being or of how an event takes place.

Material Cause

Aristotle, as he himself tells us, was the first philosopher to identify all four kinds of causes. Each cause is a different kind of answer to the question "why?" There are four kinds of answers to this question (i.e. answers which identify the matter, form, source and end). Thus, to the question, "why is this a statue?", Aristotle can give four sorts of answers: This is a statue because it is made of marble; because it is in the shape of David; because Michelangelo sculpted it; because Michelangelo wanted to depict the figure of David in marble (because he needed the money, perhaps). An account of each kind of cause is important for a fully scientific account of whatever a philosopher is explaining. Aristotle developed his account of the four causes from his analysis of change.

In every change there is, first of all, something that receives a new determination. Before undergoing the change, it is in potency to a new determination; then under the action of an efficient source it receives a new actualization. The marble upon which the sculptor works is in potency to receiving the new determination which the sculptor gives it. This new determination is the form of the statue. This example of marble receiving the form of the statue is a case accidental change, since what comes to be is a new accidental form (the **shape**) in what is already a **substance** (the marble). There are also cases of substantial change, that is, cases of new substances coming to be. Aristotle calls this kind of change generation and corruption. For example, when eat an apple, the apple stops being an apple and becomes part of me. The other principle case of substantial change occurs when any plant or animal (which is a substance) ceases to be what it was. That is, the death of an animal, for example, is a substantial change, since the corpse (a collection of substances without any cohesion) comes to be from what previously did have cohesion (a living animal). On this view, substantial changes are occurring all the time in nature, as new substances come to be by generation, and old substances pass away, by being eaten, or simply by dying and decomposing.

Since it seems that anything might ultimately change into anything else, Aristotle postulated that there is an ultimate stuff that underlies the radical potency of everything to turn into anything else. And since Aristotle calls whatever is the bearer of potency the 'matter' in any change, this ultimate stuff is called 'prime matter.' Prime matter, in its own theoretical self, is without any determination but is mere potentiality as such. This is not to say that prime matter is ever the immediate and direct subject of a change on which any actual agent acts. It exists only in actual determinate things, as the radical potency to undergo limitless changes. Prime matter is only and always found with some substantial form that gives it determination. Yet, although it is never exists in and of itself, prime matter is real; it is a real principle of change. It is the real potency that every material thing has to undergo an indefinite amount of change.

We should not, therefore, say that prime matter is the simplest bodies of the material sublunary world; the four elements, earth, air, fire and water, themselves contain contraries and can be transmuted into one another. But if they change, then they presuppose composition of potentiality and act. Air, for instance, is air, but can become fire. It has the form or actuality of air, but it also has the potentiality of becoming fire. But it is logically necessary to presuppose, prior to the potentiality of becoming fire or any other particular and definite kind of thing, a potentiality for becoming at all, i.e. a bare potentiality.

Modern nuclear physics tells us that the matter of everything can ultimately and theoretically be converted into **energy**, and energy can similarly be converted into matter. Nevertheless, there still seems to be some principle that underlies each of these two ways of being physical but cannot exist without being one or the other, matter or energy. Thus, it seems that we still have a theoretical need for the notion of prime matter.

Formal Cause

Each and every individual thing is composed not only of matter, but also of form. **Form** is the principle of determination which accounts for the thing being the kind of thing it is. As matter is the principle of potentiality, of the ability to become other than it is, form is the principle of actuality, of the thing being the sort of thing it is. In natural things, the substantial form is specifically the same for all members of the same species. That is, the substantial form of a thing accounts for it being the sort of thing it is, for belonging to the species to which it does belong. Thus, substantial form, considered apart from any matter in which it resides, is universal. Although form connotes shape or configuration, Aristotle means by form something more.

But in the case of living things, it is very clear that to explain behaviour we must refer not to surface configuration, but to the functional organization that the individuals share with other members of their species. This is the form; this, and not the shape remains the same as long as the creature is the same creature. The lion may change its shape, get thin or fat, without ceasing to be the same lion; its form is not its shape, but its soul, the set of vital capacities, the functional organization, in virtue of which it lives and acts. A corpse has the same shape as a living man; but it is not a man, since it cannot perform the activities appropriate to a man. When I ask for the formal account of lion behaviour, I am not, then, asking just for a reference to tawny colour or great weight. I am asking for an account of what it is to be a lion: how lions are organized to function, what vital capacities they have, and how these interact. And it is this, again, rather than an enumeration of its material constituents, that will provide the most simple, general, and relevant account for the scientist interested in explaining and predicting lion behaviour.

The arrangements of parts is what members of a series have in common; it is the reason that they belong to the same species. The substantial form is the cause of this arrangement; and the soul is the substantial form for living things. Aristotle, thus, is not a materialist in that he believes things cannot be reduced to their atomic constitution. Rather, Aristotle appeals to the Formal Cause to account for the reason the material constituents are arranged as they are.

Just as prime matter cannot exist without some substantial form, substantial form is not instantiated (usually) except in some material substrate. That is, for most animals, a soul cannot exist except in a body. Moreover, a soul of a certain kind (of plant or animal) can only enform a body of a certain specific type and arrangement as determined by the kind of living thing (plant or animal) whose soul makes this body to be a living body. Thus, when the body of a plant or an animal ceases to be a living body, the soul ceases to be also. To suppose that the same soul might exist as a dog, a lion and a human being would be to Aristotle and Aquinas totally incomprehensible; they do not believe in a transmigration of souls. Although the souls of almost all living things cease to exist with the death of the body, the case of the human soul presents **Aquinas** and Aristotle with certain problems.

Efficient Cause

The efficient cause of a motion may be also be internal to the thing. In natural motions the efficient cause of the motion is the natural form of the thing that changes. This applies to all the kinds of motions there are, i.e. natural alterations (an apple turning from green to red), the growth of plants and animals, and all natural local motions. This doctrine of natural motions even applies to inanimate bodies since for Aristotle and Aquinas natural bodies tend to their natural place (fire tends up, earth tends down). The internal source for the motion of growth for all living things is soul. Animals have the further motions of local motion and sensation, and the efficient cause of these motions is also soul.

Aquinas uses the notion of efficient cause in various ways in the first three of his five proofs for the existence of God. The basic line of reasoning claims that we observe effects that must have been produced by some efficient cause. That cause itself is either caused by something prior, or it is uncaused. Since there cannot be an infinite regress in essentially subordinated causes (i.e. causes that rely on prior causes to exercise their own causality), there must be some First Cause (which Aquinas believes must be God) of all the effects that follow from it. However, Aristotle believes that the world has always been in motion, and Aquinas believes, against the opinion of **St. Bonaventure**, for example, that there is no way to prove or disprove this belief in the eternity of the world from a philosophical point of view. Aquinas, therefore, believes that it is an article of faith that the world had a beginning in time. Nevertheless, he still believes that even an eternal world requires an efficient cause to sustain the motions that occur within it, and a world stretching back into an infinite past, nevertheless, leads to the same conclusion that there is a God, who is the First Cause of that infinitely old world.

The problem of the whether the eternity of the world is a philosophically necessary conclusion, and whether its truth implies the non-existence of God, were exceedingly important problems for Aquinas. So much so, that he wrote an entire work on the subject: *On the Eternity of the World.*

Final Cause

The final cause, according to Aristotle is that for the sake of which motion happens. It is the end or purpose for which the motion takes place. Again, it is easy to understand this doctrine if one considers motions which humans initiate. A sculptor sculpts in order to produce an statue, which he might do in order to make money. In nature, the final cause is not external to the thing that acts, but internal. Fruit does not grow to be food for humans and animals, but for the sake of generating another tree. Thus, typically, in generation, the final cause is the full actualization of the form, i.e. the mature adult of whatever species is generated. This doctrine has received the charge of anthropomorphism. However, for Aristotle, the fact that nature works "always or for the most part" to produce the same result is evidence that there is a genuine cause at work.

The notion of final causality is used by Aquinas as the basis for another proof for the existence of God, i.e. the Fifth Way. It should be noted, however, that the proof does NOT say that there is a purpose to the whole universe, and that this ultimate final cause is God. The proof merely asserts that something or other acts for an end which it does not know and does not choose, and that this fact shows that there is a cause of those things which directs them to their final causes. The notion of final cause is also the basis of *Thomistic Natural Law*.

Analysis of Four Causes

The study of nature was a search for answers to the question "why?" before and independently of Aristotle. A critical examination of the use of the language of causality by his predecessors, together with a careful study of natural phenomena, led Aristotle to elaborate a theory of causality. This theory is presented in its most general form in *Physics II 3* and in *Metaphysics V 5*. In both texts, Aristotle argues that a final, formal, efficient or material cause can be given in answer to a why-question.

Although Aristotle's theory of causality is developed in the context of his science of nature, its application goes well beyond the boundaries of natural science. This is already clear from the most general presentation of the theory in *Physics II 3* and in *Metaphysics V 5*. Here the four causes are used to explain human action as well as artistic production. In addition, any theoretical investigation that there might be besides natural science will employ the doctrine of the four causes.

Consider, briefly, the case of Aristotle's *Metaphysics*. Here Aristotle is seeking wisdom. Part of the argument of the *Metaphysics* is in an attempt to clarify what sort of wisdom. Aristotle is seeking. Suffice it to say that Aristotle conceives of this wisdom as a science of substance that is, or is a part of, a science of being qua being. What is important is that this science consists in a causal investigation, that is, a search for the relevant causes. This helps us to understand why the most general presentation of Aristotle's theory of causality is repeated, in almost the same words, in *Physics II 3* and in

Metaphysics V 5. Although the Physics and the Metaphysics belong to two different theoretical enterprises, in both cases we are expected to embark on an investigation that will eventuate in causal knowledge, and this is not possible without a firm grasp of the interrelations between the four types of causes.

Summary

Aristotle was not the first person to engage in a causal investigation of the world around us. From the very beginning, and independently of Aristotle, the investigation of the natural world consisted in the search for the relevant causes of a variety of natural phenomena. From the *Phaedo*, for example, we learn that the so-called "inquiry into nature" consisted in a search for "the causes of each thing; why each thing comes into existence, why it goes out of existence, why it exists". In this tradition of investigation, the search for causes was a search for answers to the question "why?". Both in the *Physics* and in the *Metaphysics* Aristotle places himself in direct continuity with this tradition. At the beginning of the *Metaphysics* Aristotle offers a concise review of the results reached by his predecessors. From this review we learn that all his predecessors were engaged in an investigation that eventuated in knowledge of one or more of the following causes: material, formal, efficient and final cause. However, Aristotle makes it very clear that all his predecessors merely touched upon these causes. That is to say, they did not engage in their causal investigation with a firm grasp of these four causes. They lacked a complete understanding of the range of possible causes and their systematic interrelations. Put differently, and more boldly, their use of causality was not supported by an adequate theory of causality. According to Aristotle, this explains why their investigation, even when it resulted in important insights, was not entirely successful.

Model Questions

1. Write a short note on *The four causes*.
2. Narrate the ideas of Aristotle on *inquiry in to nature*.
3. Write a short note on the 4th cause.

4. Aristotle held that there were four kinds of answers to "why" questions. Which are they?
5. How Aristotle's *The four causes* and Modern nuclear physics are related?
6. How Aquinas used the notion of efficient cause in various ways in the first three of his five proofs?

References

1. Annas, J., 1982, "Inefficient Causes," Philosophical Quarterly, 32: 311–322; reprinted in T. Irwin (ed.), Classical Philosophy. Collected Papers, New York/ London: Routledge, 1995, pp. 11–27.
2. Bogen, J., 1974, "Moravcsik on Explanation," Synthese, 28: 19–25.
3. Code, A., 1987, "Soul as Efficient Cause in Aristotle's Embryology," Philosophical Topics, 15: 51–59.
4. Freeland, C., 1991, "Accidental Causes and Real Explanations," in L. Judson (ed.), Aristotle's Physics: A Collection of Essays, Oxford: Oxford University Press, pp. 49–72.
5. Gourinat, J.-B., 2013, "'Origine du mouvement' et 'cause efficiente' chez Aristote," in C. Viano, C. Natali, and M. Zingano (eds.), Aitia I: Les quatres causes: origines et interpretation, Leuven: Peeters, pp. 91–119.
6. Hocutt, M., 1974, "Aristotle's Four Becauses," Philosophy, 49: 385–399.
7. http://borishennig.de/texte/2009/fourcauses.pdf
8. http://inductivequest.blogspot.com/2011/07/induction-of-aristotles-theory-of-four.html
9. http://www.aquinasonline.com/Topics/4causes.html
10. http://www.wabashcenter.wabash.edu/syllabi/c/cohen/phil320/4causes.htm
11. https://en.wikipedia.org/wiki/Four_causes
12. https://faculty.washington.edu/smcohen/433/FourCauses.pdf
13. https://plato.stanford.edu/entries/aristotle-causality/
14. https://simplyphilosophy.org/study/aristotles-four-causes/
15. https://study.com/academy/lesson/aristotles-metaphysics-the-four-causes.html
16. https://study.com/academy/lesson/aristotles-metaphysics-the-four-causes.html
17. https://www.coursera.org/lecture/management-philosophy/the-four-causes-of-aristotle-82Jig
18. Littlefield, pp. 237–246.
19. Matthen, M., 1989, "The Four Causes in Aristotle's Embryology," Apeiron (Special Issue, Nature, Knowledge and Virtue, R. Kraut and T. Penner, eds.), 22 (4): 159–180.

20. Moravcsik, J. M., 1974, "Aristotle on Adequate Explanations," Synthese, 28: 3–17.
21. Mure, G. R. G., 1975, "Cause and Because in Aristotle," Philosophy, 50: 356–357.

Index

D

E